Make a Difference

Forty Days of Repentance

By Susan Miller

Make a Difference

Forty Days of Repentance

by Susan Miller

MAKE A DIFFERENCE Forty Days of Repentance

Published by Semi-Colon Publishing, Loveland, Colorado

© 2020 by Susan Miller

Cover design by BreAnna Brown, Arizona State University, copyright © 2020.
ISBN: 978-1-7334768-7-4
Printed in the United States of America

Other Books by this Author can be found on Amazon

Three-part Messiah Series: written Myra Emslie and/or Susan Miller

Book 1. 7 Miles with Messiah - *Finding Truth in Prophecy and History*
         by Myra Emslie and Susan Miller

Book 2. 7 Days with Messiah - *Things I Didn't Learn in Sunday School*
         by Susan Miller

Book 3. 7 Hours with Messiah - *Changing Everything Forever – His Story*
         by Myra Emslie

DEDICATION

I would like to dedicate this Journey
to all those who have ever prayed some form of the sinner's prayer.

Pack your "Let's-Go-Bag" and walk with this Savior of yours
on a trip that will draw the two of you closer.

Just you and Him for forty days...
What could possibly happen?

At the end, you will know your Savior in a way you have always desired.
Jesus/Yeshua is more than a theological character.

He is God. He is Love. He is Life. He is Truth.
He is Peace. He is Joy. He is Comfort.
He is Judge. He is Real.

This book is for Grown-up-Christians of all ages.

FOREWORD

Lifetimes come and go. Days dawn and are spent, never to return again. We walk through challenges, honors and tragedies, hanging on to… what? What are we hanging on to? For some of us, we hang on to faith in the Most High God, Creator of the universe. For others it may be something else. But we all hang on to something.

When we walk through these days of our lives and finally see God as our Author, we know that we need to be right with Him somehow. But where do we go to find out how? How do we please Him? How do we hear His voice? How do we even pray to One who is utterly holy?

The answers to every profound question are found, hidden in plain sight, in the Bible. Delving into its pages of Truth brings great revelation into the Heart and Purpose and Plan of God. His Heart has plenty of room for all of us, for He loves with everlasting love.

How do we honor Him and thank Him for all He has done? One way is to take His Word seriously and do what it says to do. One thing it says to do is to search our hearts and ask the LORD to mend them and cleanse them, writing His Word upon them. That searching begins with repentance.

Susan Miller has been teaching Bible Truth for over twenty years. The hours and days and years she has spent sitting in the presence of the LORD have borne eternal fruit… both in her personal life and in her teaching. Words in the Bible that are often glossed over, are neon signs for her as she presents His profound Truth to others.

Repentance is the precious, gilded key that brings us into the Heart and Favor of God. Susan has written 40 meditations about repentance. Each one is carefully crafted to stand alone and to be considered together with the others. Each one is artfully linked with Psalms, and Scriptures from both the Old and New Testaments. Each one ends with a prayer. All of them are designed to be a place to start, a time to reflect, and a revelation of Eternal Truth.

Forty meditations, forty days, forty prayers, forty groups of Psalms… such a small number considering the magnitude of the blessings the LORD bestows on us on a regular basis. Walk with Him on this, His journey to His Heart and yours.

Your will never be sorry you did.

Myra Emslie
July 26, 2020

ACKNOWLEDGEMENTS

I would like to take this opportunity to thank my friend and fellow author, Myra Emslie. She made the comment that a series of articles I wrote should be the basis for a book. Her comment was repeated several times. After I finally listened and reworked the material, she then graciously became the editor for this project! When the editing was finished, I promised her that I would eventually learn not to end a sentence with a preposition. This work would never have come about without her dedicated encouragement. Thank you, Myra, my friend! Without you, this would have remained a series-of-emails to be deleted at the touch of a button.

I want to thank my granddaughter, BreAnna Brown for the illustration on the cover. She is gifted, not only in artistic ways, but in her ability to listen and then turn the idea into a picture worth a thousand words. She has done illustrations for four book covers thus far. She is a gift from God. Thank you, Bre, you are an incredible young woman with a very bright future.

Thanks to the Pixabay contributors for the pictures included in this book. They provide an invaluable service!

TABLE OF CONTENTS

INTRODUCTION

We are all familiar with the American adage of the **3-R's** of last century's school-yard-days: '**R**eadin', '**R**itin' and '**R**ithmatic'. If you grew up on a ranch, there were two more: '**R**idin' and '**R**opin'. Becoming competent in at least three of these five areas would pretty much assure you a successful life.

In the Bible, the Big-**R**-Word is REPENTANCE…
What is it? How do we do it? When do we do it? Why do we do it? Where do we do it?

Look at the modern online definition of **Repentance**:
> *The action of repenting; sincere regret or remorse.*

Look at the Biblical definition of **Repentance**:
> *To cause to return, bring back, allow to return, restore, relinquish, give in payment.*

If we combine the *On-Line-definition* and the *Biblical-definition* of **Repentance,** we have: *a sincere regret **and** a cause to return to the Covenant with God that is available for us.*

The Biblical definition of Repentance is talking about returning to God **and** His ways **and** His Word **and** His Covenant. The God of the Bible is the God of Israel. Being adopted is the only way to become a member of His family. If you are adopted into His family, then you are of Israel too. (read Romans 11:11-31 for a refresher)

It is very good news, when we find out that we do not need to be separated from God. He desires a relationship with us. But it involves our desire to *turn* or *return* to Him.

The following pages will address and help us understand the word, ***Repentance***. Gentle Reader, Repentance is more than, "I'm sorry for my sins." Yes, we are… and yes, we are forgiven. But God has more for us to understand about His wonderous mercy, and about Him welcoming us back into His Presence, and under His Wings, and into His Family. Let's take the time to consider His Ways.

There is a period of time on God's calendar that includes 40-Days-of-Repentance. Most Christians don't know of this. We find these days and months on a Hebrew calendar. These 40 days include the 6th month of Elul, and the first ten days of the 7th month of Tishri.

The first ten days counted in Tishri, begin with Yom Teruah (Day of Trumpets), and end with Yom Kippur (Day of Atonement), which falls on the tenth day of the month. These ten days, by themselves, are referred to as the Days of Awe. Jewish people see this as the Books of Judgment are open on Yom Teruah and the practicing Jew, wants to be sure his/her name is written in the Book of Life by Yom Kippur… each year. It is the season to make sure that relationships are right.

I know and you know the soul of the Christian is atoned for by the blood of Jesus, and our sins are forgiven. The blood of bulls and goats and lambs are no longer required, and our names are written in the Lamb's Book of Life. Halleluyah! However, understanding the need for and the power of repentance, and humbling ourselves before a Holy God is another topic altogether.

We Christians can get very cavalier about day-to-day responsibilities in living a life of justice, righteousness and mercy. We still are responsible to God for our character and our conduct, right? To understand the meaning behind *II Chronicles 7:14* is crucial in the generation we are now in. *If My people, who are called by My Name will humble themselves and pray, then will I hear from heaven and heal their land.*

This book will lead the reader through a 40-day journey of meditations on repentance. It doesn't have to be according to the Jewish calendar. God welcomes the company every day, every week, every month.

We, the American Christian, as a group, have a National Mandate from our founding fathers:

- to be the city on the hill with a light for all nations;
- to be the land from where the Good News of the Gospel is supposed to reach the ends of the earth;
- to be the good big brother to the rest of the nations; and
- to be the nation that shows the world what freedom looks like.

Two British ministers (Reed and Matheson) visiting America in 1834 penned the following words in a subsequent book: "America will be great if America is good. If not, her greatness will vanish away like a morning cloud." It is now less than 200 years later. Are we in danger of vanishing like the morning fog?

My fellow Christian, those assignments from our founding fathers are not up to: the government, the sports and entertainment industry, business, the schools, or the media.

God put the individual family in charge of deciding how things would be run in this country! Think about it.

It's from the bottom up… not from the top down. We are not to be a nation with a human king or tyrant ruling over us. The true responsibility of this country is with the dads and moms. They are charged with raising children: to respect others, to have a reverence for God, to be aware of what is being taught in their children's schools, to be sure of what and who is entertaining their kids. Of course, we must also be astute as to who is running for public office and what they stand for. Parents were to do this job by the grace of God dwelling in their midst. How are we doing? That is a rhetorical question and we all know the answer.

Our nation is in a quagmire today. Where do we start? Who do we trust? Is this where we call upon II Chronicles 7:14? It's a good place to start. We need some meditation and instruction of just how we can approach God - both in humility, and confidence… that He cares enough to hear our prayers and heal our land.

Is Forty a significant number in the Bible? We can list a few people associated with the number 40:

- **Noah,**
- **Moses,**
- **Joshua and Caleb,**
- **David,**
- **Solomon,**
- **Jesus,**
- **First generation of Christian up to 70 AD.**

So, 40 Days of Repentance, huh? What can you expect from 40 days of Repentance? Allow me to explain. It doesn't matter when you start counting the 40 days. There is always room to spend time with God. He loves it and keeps waiting. Just do it… start today and see what happens 40 days from now.

Let's try to understand the culture of the Jewish person doing this each year, according to the Jewish calendar. If we start on the first day of the sixth Hebrew month (Elul) and count 40 days, we would end up at the Day of Atonement… the tenth day of the seventh month. Briefly, the Day of Atonement (or Yom Kippur) is as important to the Jewish Community as Resurrection Day is to Christians.

The sixth month of the Hebrew calendar is called, Elul. It is when the season of reaping crops begins. The root of this word, in Hebrew, means, to *search*. What better time to *search* out what we have sown into the world over the past season?

This important time occurs during the hot days of summer - the days of Harvest. While waiting for the crops and the fruits to gather, it is also a time of *reflection*, *repentance* and *repairing* things with the people you might be at odds with since the last time you went through this process. That is why these 40 days are generally known as the Days of Repentance.

If this is your first time to follow a journey, then welcome! It's a time to get in touch with your inner-man for a self-assessment. This is the 'reaping-what-you-have-sown' days.

Let's take this journey of harvest together. Let's do it one-day-at-a-time and perhaps discover some new and refreshing things about our Relationship with God. Who knows? Maybe we will grow closer to Him? God knows! He really does want us to take, "Yes" for an answer and that is something we need to practice. "Yes"- we are forgiven… and, "Yes" - we have a reason for living… in the freedom and enjoyment of His Truth.

If possible, read *Psalm 27* each day during this journey with your Abba.
It will encourage and enlighten you!

An Exuberant Declaration of Faith

A Psalm of David

27 The LORD is my light and my salvation; Whom shall I fear?
The LORD is the strength of my life; Of whom shall I be afraid?
² When the wicked came against me To eat up my flesh,
My enemies and foes, They stumbled and fell.
³ Though an army may encamp against me, My heart shall not fear;
Though war may rise against me, In this I will be confident.

⁴ One thing I have desired of the LORD, That will I seek:
That I may dwell in the house of the LORD All the days of my life,
To behold the beauty of the LORD, And to inquire in His temple.
⁵ For in the time of trouble He shall hide me in His pavilion;
In the secret place of His tabernacle He shall hide me;
He shall set me high upon a rock.

⁶ And now my head shall be lifted up above my enemies all around me;
Therefore I will offer sacrifices of joy in His tabernacle; I will sing, yes, I will sing
praises to the LORD.

⁷ Hear, O LORD, when I cry with my voice! Have mercy also upon me, and answer me.
⁸ When You said, "Seek My face," My heart said to You, "Your face, LORD, I will seek."
⁹ Do not hide Your face from me; Do not turn Your servant away in anger;
You have been my help; Do not leave me nor forsake me,
O God of my salvation. ¹⁰ When my father and my mother forsake me,
Then the LORD will take care of me.

¹¹ Teach me Your way, O LORD, And lead me in a smooth path, because of my enemies.
¹² Do not deliver me to the will of my adversaries; For false witnesses have risen against
me, And such as breathe out violence. ¹³ I would have lost heart, unless I had believed
That I would see the goodness of the LORD In the land of the living.

¹⁴ Wait on the LORD; Be of good courage, And He shall strengthen your heart;
Wait, I say, on the LORD! (NIV)

Make a Difference
Forty Days of Repentance

Day 1

Moses on the Mountain/Yeshua with the Sheep

On this day, (what would become the first day of Elul) Moses ascended Mt. Sinai again for 40 days, to plead with God to continue taking the Children of Israel to the Land of Promise. On top of the mountain, God reveals something very special to Moses describing Himself this way:

> "The Lord, the Lord God, merciful and gracious, longsuffering and abounding in goodness and truth, ⁷ keeping mercy for thousands, forgiving iniquity and transgression and sin, by no means clearing the guilty, visiting the iniquity of the fathers upon the children and the children's children to the third and the fourth generation." Exodus 34:6-7

On this same day two thousand years later, Yeshua was moved by compassion when He saw the multitudes as sheep with no Shepherd. He said to the Disciples,

> "The harvest truly is plentiful, but the laborers are few." Matthew 9:37

Examine me, O LORD, and prove me; try my mind and my heart... Psalm:26:2

Psalms 1-3 are the suggested reading for today

Here is a taste

Psalm 2

[10]Now therefore, be wise, O kings; Be instructed, you judges of the earth.
[11]Serve the Lord with fear, And rejoice with trembling.
[12]Kiss the Son, lest He be angry, And you perish in the way,
When His wrath is kindled but a little.
Blessed are all those who put their trust in Him.

Abba,

You are gracious and full of Truth. As I begin this forty-day journey with You, I commit to spend my 'currency of time' with You, and before You. I want this time to be invested in knowing You. Please speak to my heart, teach me about You and about me. Thank You for the forgiveness that You have extended to me.

Amen

Day 2

Clean and Repair a Broken Vessel

The month of Elul and the first ten days of Tishri are akin to cleaning and repairing a broken vessel. We have the assurance that God is working in us to rebuild; however, this is not a passive exercise. God wants to partner with you to bring healing and wholeness into your life. We are the ones that must make righteous decisions, and draw near to Him in an atmosphere of repentance, and with a desire to turn toward Him. The abundant life will follow.

But seek first the Kingdom of God and His righteousness,
and all these things will be added unto you. Matthew 6:33

Psalms 4-6 are the suggested reading for today

Here is a taste

Psalm 4:2-3

How long, O you sons of men,
Will you turn my glory to shame?
How long will you love worthlessness
And seek falsehood? Selah
3 But know that the Lord has set apart for Himself him who is godly;
The Lord will hear when I call to Him.

Abba… You have found and rescued me. You are taking the broken pieces of my life and mending them. We have loved the wrong things and sought after the worthless. You are the lifter of my head. Create in me something beautiful and useful in Your Kingdom. Make me a vessel in Your hands. Fill me with Your Spirit and pour me out for Your glory.

Amen

Day 3

The Elul Zone

The month of Elul, an Akkadian word from Babylon meaning *harvest*, is a time of heart searching, which comes from a similar word in Aramaic, meaning *search*. Thus, it has become a time of *searching* one's heart during *harvest* time. Harvest time should be a joyous time of reaping what has been growing in our life during the past year as well as preparing for next year's crop.

Life happens in measurements of years… one-year-at-a-time. Remembering that the Farmer said, *"let the wheat and tares grow together until the time of the harvest,"* should sound familiar. The good crop of wheat will be full of grain, bowing in the wind… even as we bow in thanksgiving to God. The tares, (aka weeds), will be standing tall, as if proud, but empty with nothing of substance to offer the Farmer. While growing, wheat and tares will look alike, until the tares are found out to be weeds.

Weed-pulling is what we should be doing. Searching, repenting and allowing the tares we have growing in our own "garden" to be pulled up and out of our own field. Will the good crop will be ready to be brought into the storehouse?

[24] Another parable He put forth to them, saying: "The kingdom of heaven is like a man who sowed good seed in his field; [25] but while men slept, his enemy came and sowed tares among the wheat and went his way. [26] But when the grain had sprouted and produced a crop, then the tares also appeared. [27] So the servants of the owner came and said to him, 'Sir, did you not sow good seed in your field? How then does it have tares?' [28] He said to them, 'An enemy has done this.' The servants said to him, 'Do you want us then to go and gather them up?' [29] But he said, 'No, lest while you gather up the tares you also uproot the wheat with them. [30] Let both grow together until the harvest, and at the time of harvest I will say to the reapers, "First gather together the tares and bind them in bundles to burn them, but gather the wheat into my barn."'" Matthew 13:24-30

Isaiah spoke of the work of John the Baptist in chapter 40:3-5. John was the rightful heir to the Levitical Priesthood and he took his teaching out to the wilderness.

The voice of one crying in the wilderness: "Prepare the way of the Lord; Make straight in the desert A highway for our God. [4] Every valley shall be exalted and every mountain and hill brought low; The crooked places shall be made straight and the rough places smooth; [5] The glory of the Lord shall be revealed, And all flesh shall see it together; For the mouth of the Lord has spoken." Isaiah 40:3-5

Look at John the Baptist's teaching in Luke 3. He had some wise things to say about repentance to different groups of people coming to him asking what they should do. What did repentance look like for: the common people; the tax collectors; the soldiers?

- To the people: SHARE… your clothing and food
- To the tax collectors: BE HONEST... do not steal
- To the soldiers: DO NOT ACCUSE ANYONE FALSELY and BE CONTENT especially with your wages

Micah 6:8
What does the LORD require of you?

- *DO JUSTICE*
- *LOVE KINDNESS*
- *WALK HUMBLY WITH YOUR GOD*

Psalms 7-9 are the suggested reading for today

Here is a taste

O enemy, destructions are finished forever! And you have destroyed cities;
Even their memory has perished. But the Lord shall endure forever;
He has prepared His throne for judgment.
He shall judge the world in righteousness,
And He shall administer judgment for the peoples in uprightness.
Psalm 9: 6-8

Abba… Help me to lift up my eyes and see what You see and what You require: justice, kindness, humilty. As Your people, we love the fairness of Your justice. As Your child, I love the benefit of Your kindness. As Your servant, I desire to walk with a humble spirit, unpretenciously before You. What wonderdful qualites to desire: justice, kindness, unpretenciousness.

Amen

Day 4

Accounting for the Past - Preparing for the Future

There is an old Jewish proverb, "Your future lies behind you."

In this month of Elul, how we go about accounting for the past is how we prepare for the future. The Aramaic meaning of the word Elul is 'searching'. This allows for examining the mistakes of the year in order not to repeat them, and doing so with a heart of humility.

> *Examine me, O LORD, and prove me; try my mind and my heart. Psalm 26:2*

The Bible has answers to perplexing questions… provided that we look. You will find answers from every dark place that threatens to envelop you, or from every attack that comes your way. Psalm 27 says that God is Light. Light will banish the darkness each and every time. Remember, the Jewish people are reading Psalm 27 twice a day during this time period... and it sounds like a good idea!)

> *The LORD is my light and my salvation; whom shall I fear? The LORD is the strength of my life. Psalm 27:1*

> *This is the message we heard from Jesus and now declare to you: God is light, and there is no darkness in him at all. ⁶ So we are lying if we say we have fellowship with God but go on living in spiritual darkness; we are not practicing the truth. ⁷ But if we are living in the light, as God is in the light, then we have fellowship with each other, and the blood of Jesus, his Son, cleanses us from all sin. I John 1:5-7 (NLT)*

Ask the Holy Spirit to shine His light into dark corners of your life; allowing Him to begin banishing away every dark thing.

Are you being tested? Are you facing a trial of some kind? If so, then consider yourself part of the family! Everyone is undergoing some kind of *test* to some degree or another.

Don't waste the energy wishing circumstances away. There are powerful forces at work. This is the time to remember your First Love and the Promise of the Father to send the Comforter. Press in, hang on, believing that He is working all things for good.

Remember that you are insufficient in your own strength to handle your troubles by yourself. You have the Holy Spirit living within you to help in times of trouble, and with Him, you can handle anything. If you view your circumstances from the Big-Picture-Perspective, you can have joy in the midst of struggles or troubles.

Patience, Prudence, Perseverance are watchwords for these days… and these words can be your friends as the Holy Spirit completes His work in you. BIG PICTURE; BIG SIGNS; BIG ANSWERS… will come to those whose hearts are steadfastly trusting Him.

Psalm 10 is the suggested reading for today

Here is a taste

Lord, You have heard the desire of the humble;
You will prepare their heart;
You will cause Your ear to hear,
To do justice to the fatherless and the oppressed,
That the man of the earth may oppress no more. Psalm 10: 17-18

Abba… Thank You that I am not walking this journey alone. You are with me. It is easy to see the iniquity of the nations and your enemies each day. Corruption is everywhere, but I don't want anything to do with it. I want You to draw near and mend this heart of mine. I want iniquity and separateness to be far from me. Thank You for the blood of Jesus that cleanses us from sin and shame. Thank You for Your Word that cleanses and sets us free from the corruption. Help me to represent You today, to reflect You and Your love for others.

Amen

Day 5

God is King and Father and Judge

In Deuteronomy 16, God calls for a system of judges to be instituted. God expects His people to live within community, and with a system of law and order. Worshiping God is imperative as witnessed by the Torah. It is our duty to Worship Him. God is all about Mercy… and He is all about Justice as well. In this same chapter, we are introduced to Cities of Refuge. God provides a way and a place for those who repent and return to Him.

> *He will judge the world in righteousness, and He shall administer judgment for the peoples in uprightness. Psalm 9:8*

> *The name of the Lord is **a strong tower;** The righteous run to it and are safe. Prov. 18:10*

~~

We are living in a world where love is growing cold… even though the two commandments that Yeshua emphasized from the Torah are: Love the LORD your God with all your heart, soul and might, **and** love one another. The Gospel writers: Matthew (22), Mark (12) and Luke (10) all agree. That is the focus of this season of repentance.

If we are doing this, or attempting to do this… then we are on the right track. His love for us is unfailing. It is vital to remember that Yeshua is: the Creator of life; the Sustainer of the universe; our Savior, our Brother, our Friend… and yes, our Judge. There is an ancient Jewish commentary that says, "When you appear for Divine Judgment, the angels will say to you: 'Fear not, the Judge is your Father.'" This Courtroom is where we are headed; that the Judge is our Father is very reassuring. We know we are not alone. As we walk in His Light and in His Presence, He will sing over us with joy!

[16] On that day the announcement to Jerusalem will be, "Cheer up, Zion! Don't be afraid!
[17] For the Lord your God is living among you He is a mighty savior.
He will take delight in you with gladness. With his love, he will calm all your fears.
He will rejoice over you with joyful songs." Zephaniah 3:16-18 NLT

Psalms 10-12 are the suggested reading for today

Here is a taste

The LORD is King forever and ever; The nations have perished out of His land.
[17] LORD, You have heard the desire of the humble; You will prepare their heart;
You will cause Your ear to hear,[18] To do justice to the fatherless and the oppressed,
That the man of the earth may oppress no more. Psalm 10: 16-18

Abba… You are the King and the Judge and my Father. Thank You for accepting me into You Kingdom. Help me to realize that I am walking in Your Kingdom each day. I want to represent You in the way You expect of Your children. You are God and I am Yours.

Amen

Blessings and Saleh

Day 6

Three Pillars, Two Foundations

"But if, when you arrive in the land the Lord will give you, there are any among you who are poor, you must not shut your heart or hand against them; 8 you must lend them as much as they need. Deuteronomy 15:7   NLT

The Jewish sages say that the world rests on THREE PILLARS: *Torah; Prayer; and Kindness* through Charity. Also, there are TWO FOUNDATIONS: *Repentance and Redemption.* During this time of soul searching all of these are emphasized: **Pillars and Foundations**. Through acts of charity, we become givers and not just takers. It is important to give of *time,* and *energy* and *resources.* This is not just an act of charity; it is DOING what is *just* and *right*… completing the cycle of *give* and *take* in the Kingdom.

Helping is part of the internal workings of God's Kingdom. It should come natural to God's family of Believers to help. How can I help? What can I do to help? Notice the verse identifies where giving starts… in the heart. We are commanded to not 'shut our hearts' toward the poor, the foreigner living in our midst (as one of us), the widow, the fatherless.

During the reign of King Josiah, God said through the prophet Jeremiah: *"He judged the cause of the poor and needy; then it was well with him: was not this to know me? declares the LORD." Jeremiah 22:16.* Giving, charity and compassion are a part of God's nature and God's children should reflect this.

Note: These days-of-repentance come after the difficult commemoration of the 9th of Av; when both temples were destroyed. Many other tragic events of Jewish history happened on this day because of the sin and corruption of the people. These 40-days-of-repentance are days when one draws close unto God feeling the consolation that He has to give to His own who return to Him.

If we are spiritually asleep during this time, we will miss all that is available to us: like the comfort of a loving Father wrapping His arms around us, and welcoming us back home. For that matter, do we even stop to think about what He has in store for those who return to Him? If we did, we would run, not walk, to those awaiting arms… in humility.

All too often we think of repentance as a bad thing. It is not! It is a cleansing, healing, and comforting time to be close to the One who loves you most!

Psalms 13-15 are the suggested reading for today

Here is a taste

Have all the workers of iniquity no knowledge,
who eat up my people as they eat bread, and do not call on the Lord?
There they are in great fear, for God is with the generation of the righteous.
You shame the counsel of the poor,
but the Lord is his refuge.
Psalm 14:4-6

It is customary to increase giving during this time. In Jewish thought, no one is too poor to show loving-kindness in action to others.

Do I have a heart to help others? What can I eliminate or cut back on in order to give more to those in need?

Abba,

I realize and recognize that I really am Your child and a member of Your Kingdom. I want You to reveal to me more ways to help others who are on the way into Your Kingdom, or are already members in good standing. You are a good-good Father. Show me how to help.

Amen

Blessings and Selah

Day 7

The Blood Barrier

[11] This is all the more urgent, for you know how late it is; time is running out. Wake up, for our salvation is nearer now than when we first believed. Romans 13:11 NLT

The alarms are ringing... the days before us are serious. These *are the days* and *this is the time* to be fully awake. And to help, the shofar is blown every day in Israel during this month of Elul. Why not here in your hometown? Should we not be doing that? Can you imagine someone blowing the shofar on your street corner every morning for a month? Would that cause you and your family and your city to awaken?

The shofar is to get your attention and to call the people for a special purpose. If there ever is a month on the Hebrew calendar to call out to God... this is it!

Don't think of God as being in a bad mood during this time of Repentance. He is delighted when any of His children think on these things, search for Him and return to Him. We have a blood Covenant established with Him.

Remember the altars in the Old Testament, that consumed a substitution sacrifice with its blood poured out on the altar and the ground? Who knows how many perfect and innocent animals had their blood shed serving as a barrier between man's sin and God's holiness? I can't even imagine the amount of blood that was shed. That blood formed a barrier between the sin of men and God.

And then it happened... Yeshua came as the last blood sacrifice that would ever be required.

Remember, this month is also known as a time of consolation.... (or relief, or solace, or support).

Read Hebrews 10

The words are indeed words of consolation and comfort and must go with this month's message to us.

Look carefully at:

Yeshua's testimony beginning in v. 8

> *⁸ First, Christ said, "You did not want animal sacrifices or sin offerings or burnt offerings or other offerings for sin, nor were you pleased with them" (though they are required by the law of Moses). ⁹ Then he said, "Look, I have come to do your will." He cancels the first covenant in order to put the second into effect. ¹⁰ For God's will was for us to be made holy by the sacrifice of the body of Jesus Christ, once for all time. TLB*

The Holy Spirit's testimony beginning in v. 15:

> *¹⁵ And the Holy Spirit also testifies that this is so. For he says, ¹⁶ "This is the new covenant I will make with my people on that day,[c] says the Lord: I will put my laws in their hearts, and I will write them on their minds   Hebrews 10: 8-10; 15-18   TLB*

All of a sudden, the phrase, *pleading the blood of Jesus over us,* makes a lot more sense. He laid down His life, and His blood was shed for us 2000 years ago. We should think on that on a daily basis. "Pleading His blood" reminds us of the blood barrier that is between our sin and God's Presence. Indeed, it is what allows us into His Presence! Oh, the blood of Jesus! Thank You, Abba for such an extravagant and wonderful gift. His blood is the only thing on this earth that did not come from the earth. His blood was splashed all over the city of Jerusalem and on the hill of Calvary. It was shed for our salvation, our sanctification, and our justification. Declare it! Claim it! Use it! Remember it! His blood means eternal life for us! Halleluyah!

Psalms 16-18 are the suggested reading for today

Here is a taste

⁶ I have called upon You, for You will hear me, O God;
Incline Your ear to me, and hear my speech.
⁷ Show Your marvelous lovingkindness by Your right hand,
O You who save those who trust in You from those who rise up against them.
⁸ Keep me as the apple of Your eye.
Hide me under the shadow of Your wings,
⁹ from the wicked who oppress me,
from my deadly enemies who surround me.
Psalm 17:6-9

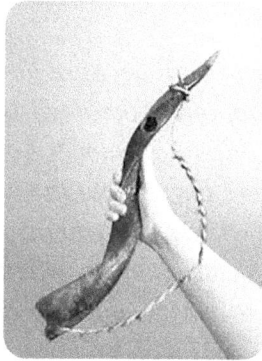

Abba… Thank You for the sound of the shofar; calling us to attention and calling us to Yourself. May we hear Your call and may we do what You ask us to do. We are so grateful for Yeshua's blood, so willingly poured out. We plead the blood of Yeshua over us, our families, our cities, our states, our country and to all the places in the world that His blood was shed for.

Amen

Day 8

US and Israel / Covenant Friends

*Turn all your anxiety over to God because he cares for you. **8** Keep your mind clear, and be alert. Your opponent the devil is prowling around like a roaring lion as he looks for someone to devour. **9** Be firm in the faith and resist him, knowing that other believers throughout the world are going through the same kind of suffering. **10** God, who shows you his kindness and who has called you through Christ Jesus to his eternal glory, will restore you, strengthen you, make you strong, and support you as you suffer for a little while. **11** Power belongs to him forever. Amen. I Peter 5:7*

There is a story about President Truman and the founding of Israel that is irresistible and charming, and has God's fingerprints all over it! It was God who caused Truman to become Vice President, just prior to the death of President Roosevelt, toward the end of WWII. (FDR and Truman had only met one time).

At the time of Israel becoming a nation: all parties, political factions, cabinet members, and power houses were opposed to there being a Jewish homeland. The world focus was on rebuilding Europe and not offending the Arab oil producers.

Truman's personal lawyer was his friend and a student of the Bible. Another of Truman's friends was a Jewish man, Eddie Jacobson. Truman and Jacobson were both from the same hometown in Missouri. Truman and Jacobson had spent a lot of time together in trench warfare during WWI. After the war they went into business, opening a haberdashery in Kansas City, Mo. These two friends of President Truman stood with him, and even changed his mind about backing a homeland for the Jews, against mighty pressure from the powers-that-be. It was President Truman, on the advice and of his Christian friend and Jewish friend, that caused America to back Israel being birthed in a day… against all human odds.

On May 14, 1948 - David Ben Gurion read the Declaration of Independence and named this reborn country, *Israel*. And 11 minutes later, Truman was the first World Leader to acknowledge it. There have been wars and rumors of wars in Israel ever since, but there is a Land called Israel once again; all because two men, one from "Judah" and one from "Joseph" stood together against all odds. Is that when the two sticks mentioned in Ezekiel 37 came together? That is courage. That is statesmanship. That is loyalty. That is an example of God's overall strategy. That is, "Shema Israel" - Hear and Do! America and Israel are linked by Covenant. And that makes Israel and the United States Covenant Friends.

Psalms 19-20 are the suggested reading for today

Here is a taste

The fear of the Lord is clean,
enduring forever;
The judgments of the Lord are true and righteous altogether.
More to be desired are they than gold,
Yea, than much fine gold;
Sweeter also than honey and the honeycomb.
Moreover by them Your servant is warned,
And in keeping them there is great reward.
Psalm 19: 9-11

Picture of Israel's Declaration of Independence... acknowledged by President Truman only 11 minutes after Ben Gurion read it to the world. Those signatures at the bottom were signed before it was even written. That is trust!

Can a land be born in one day? Can a nation be born all at once?

Stand firm and do the right thing! Don't panic nor fear... It is time to be steadfast in your faith for your family, your country, and your God.

Truman went on to win the election in November. Even though his party split into three factions. He was God's man for the hour to bless Israel. The people of America spoke louder than the politics.

"I will bless those who bless you…. and I will curse those who curse you," said God to Abraham.

Abba…

You have given Your people their homeland. For the first time in two-thousand years, the Jewish people are on the soil that You provided for them. Open their eyes, to their Messiah. You have brought them home, visit them and invite them into Your Kingdom.

Amen

Day 9

The King Returns from a Long Journey

The earth is the LORD's and all its fullness,
the world and those who dwell therein.   Psalm 24:1

"Lord God of Israel, there is no God in heaven above or
on earth below like You, who keep Your covenant and mercy with
Your servants who walk before You with all their hearts. I Kings 8:23

The sages have a story that speaks of a king returning from a long trip. He went out to see his kingdom and stood in his field greeting the people. This was the opportunity for his people to petition him without a formal audience… to go over to him and say, "hello" and even to ask for anything he or she needs. The king is smiling. He is glad to be back home and he is predisposed to grant all requests.

The Rabbis say that this story describes the month of Elul. By Yom Teruah, the King is back on His throne. Nice to know that you don't have to wait around until Yom Teruah or Yom Kippur. Go out to meet Him now. He is outstanding in His field...in every way... and He is waiting for you to drop by and say something!

Psalms 22-24 are the suggested reading for today

Here is a taste

The earth is the Lord's, and everything in it. The world and all its people belong to him. ² For he laid the earth's foundation on the seas and built it on the ocean depths. ³ Who may climb the mountain of the Lord? Who may stand in his holy place? ⁴ Only those whose hands and hearts are pure, who do not worship idols and never tell lies. ⁵ They will receive the Lord's blessing and have a right relationship with God their savior.
Psalm 24:1-5

The above story sounds like Yeshua's parable of the Talents in **Matthew 25** and **Luke 19.** Yeshua just told the *rest of the story*. These rabbinical stories from the sages have been around a long time... and Yeshua served up many of them... with a twist! This is your King... go out to meet Him. He is waiting to talk with you!

Abba...

How wonderful it would be to go out to meet You in Your field. I know I would be welcome. I know what I would ask of You. I would ask You to pour Your Spirit out across the land and give us the gift of Repentance and turn us toward You once again. O Yeshua, come quickly and establish Your throne in our midst. You are a wonderful God. Who wouldn't want to serve You?

Amen

Day 10

An Exuberant Declaration of Faith

Remember, Psalm 27 is recited twice a day during this month. This declaration, twice a day, is like putting the offering on the altar in the morning and again, prior to the evening. These words can be a *proclamation* and a *winning-combination* when pleading the blood of Yeshua over your life as you proceed through the day!

A *Psalm* of David: Psalm 27

> *27 The Lord is my light and my salvation; Whom shall I fear? The Lord is the strength of my life; Of whom shall I be afraid? 2 When the wicked came against me to eat up my flesh, my enemies, and foes, they stumbled and fell.*

> *3 Though an army may encamp against me,* **My heart shall not fear**; *Though war may rise against me In this I will confident. 4 One thing I have desired of the Lord,* **That will I seek:** *That I may dwell in the house of the Lord all the days of my life, to behold the beauty of the Lord, and to inquire in His temple.*

> *5 For in the time of trouble He shall hide me in His pavilion; In the secret place of His tabernacle He shall hide me; He shall set me high upon a rock. 6 And now my head shall be lifted up above my enemies all around me; Therefore I will offer sacrifices of joy in His tabernacle; I will sing, yes, I will* **sing praises to the Lord**. *7 Hear, O Lord, when I cry with my voice! Have mercy also upon me, and answer me.*

> *8 When You said, "Seek My face,"* **My heart said to You, "Your face, Lord, I will seek**." *9 Do not hide Your face from me; Do not turn Your servant away in anger; You have been my help; Do not leave me nor forsake me, O God of my salvation. 10 When my father and my mother forsake me, then the Lord will take care of me.*

11 Teach me Your way, O Lord, and lead me in a smooth path, because of my enemies.12 Do not deliver me to the will of my adversaries; For false witnesses have risen against me, and such as breathe out violence.13 **I would have lost heart, unless I had believed** *that I would see the goodness of the Lord in the land of the living.14 Wait on the Lord; Be of good courage, And* **He shall strengthen your heart***; Wait, I say, on the Lord!*

Closer examination of this Psalm leads us to see, once again, the importance of our heart.

- **Fear not;**
- **Seek His face;**
- **Sing praises to the Lord**
- **Don't lose heart;**
- **Believe His word and**
- **He will strengthen your heart.**

Our hearts are very important to Him. It is from the heart that feelings originate… not like your mind, where thoughts originate.

Light, Salvation, and Strength of heart all come from the LORD. Yeshua is the Light in a dark world. He is our Salvation. He is Strong and Mighty to help us in the presence of the enemy.

Once again this is about the importance of the secret place… the Holy Place. The Tabernacle reserved for the Priests of Yah; the place and position He called His people, Israel to be. What a privilege… to be called into the Secret Place of the Tabernacle. Remember it is a picture of our heart, where we can see the light, eat the bread, and speak to Him in prayer at the altar of incense.

Psalms 25-27 are suggested reading for today

Here is a taste

To You, O Lord, I lift up my soul.
2 O my God, I trust in You;
Let me not be ashamed;
Let not my enemies triumph over me.
3 Indeed, let no one who waits on You be ashamed;
Let those be ashamed who deal treacherously without cause.
Psalm 25:1-3

Abba…

You are my light and salvation and strength. Without You, there is no hope. Please forgive all my wrongs. Thank You for the wonderful gift of eternal Life. Help me be an instrument of your love and light to shine on others.

Amen

Day 11

The Unfortunate Golden Calf Incident

God describes Himself to Moses in Exodus 34: 6-7

> *6 The Lord passed by before him, and proclaimed, "The LORD, the LORD God, merciful and gracious, slow to anger, and abounding in goodness and truth, 7 keeping mercy for thousands, forgiving iniquity and transgression and sin, but who will by no means clear the guilty, visiting the iniquity of fathers on the children and on the children's children, to the third and the fourth generation."*

Of course, these words are spoken after the unfortunate golden calf incident of Exodus 32. God's heart has been broken by His bride-nation who had said, "yes" to Him just 3 months prior. God had told Moses to take the people up to the land promised to Abraham, but that He would not go with them. Moses pleaded on behalf of the people and ministered to the heart of YHVH, saying that unless God went with them to the land of their Inheritance, how would this people be any different than any other people group on the earth? Moses ministered to God's wounded heart for 40 days!

God then relented. He would indeed go with Moses and the people. The Relationship was back on! God then proclaimed 13 things about Himself in these verses of Exodus. Can you count them?

Wait - did you only count 10?

> Merciful
> Gracious
> Slow to anger
> Abounding in goodness
> Abounding in truth
> Keeping mercy
> Forgiving iniquity
> Forgiving transgressions
> Forgiving iniquity
> However, though He forgives, there will be consequences to the 3rd and 4th generation.

The Rabbis say even His Name… **YHVH, YHVH, God** counts as three. For Believers, can we see the aspects of God in those proclamations? **The Father, the Son, the Holy Spirit.**

Remember, that all of the generation who came out of Egypt, and were over twenty years of age, perished in the wilderness except two: Joshua, the man from Ephraim (son of Joseph) and Caleb, the man from Judah. These two men followed God's lead taking the next generations into the land of their inheritance. The descendants of Joseph and Judah have had a profound effect on the world!

Question: Is it important to believe God, seek His Face, hear His Voice, and stay close to Him?

Today's Psalms 28-30 seem to emphasize that the dead don't praise YHVH. It is God who saves, giving us salvation. Our mouths should be filled often, offering prayers and songs of Praise to Him. Tend to and appreciate your relationship with the LORD, even more than you would tend a lovely, healthy, fragrant flowering plant in your garden. This relationship with Him is the most precious thing you possess… a thing of beauty and a joy forever! Only God can take the pain of the past and transform it, through forgiveness, to love others. That is why He wants us to forgive those who have caused pain in our lives.

While I live will I praise the LORD:
I will sing praises unto my God while I have any being. Psalm 146:2

Psalms 28-30 are the suggested reading for today

Here is a taste

The Lord is the strength of His people,
And He is the saving refuge of His anointed.
[9] Save Your people,
And bless Your inheritance;
Shepherd them also,
And bear them up forever.

Psalm 28:8-9

Abba… Forgive us for not showing You the appreciation due to the Creator. You are the King enthroned on High and Forever! You are God and can splinter the trees of Lebanon with Your voice! You are God and we are not! We give You the glory that is due Your Name… the Name that is above every name. All of us who make up Your Temple say, "Glory and Honor to our King." Amen

Day 12

He Is God & We Are Not

REDEEMED

This Elul Zone, if you remember, is based on two things: Redemption and Repentance. These two things lead us to drawing near to God, and it is God who offers Consolation and Comfort to His people. We are always looking for two things to join together. Repentance is not just a momentary happenstance. Repentance is a process. While it can be granted in a moment... getting to that moment involves a *turn-around in behavior* and a *change of mind.*

> *Blessed is he whose transgression is forgiven; whose sin is covered. Blessed is the man to whom the LORD does not impute iniquity, and in whose spirit, there is no deceit. Psalm 32:1-2*

Now is the time to ask, **"Do I fear the LORD?"** He tells us in His word about 365 times, and in different ways, "Don't be afraid" for He is with us in many ways. However, we should have a very healthy *respect for* and *reverence for* Him. This is the One who spoke everything into existence and holds everything in the universe together and who asks us to believe and obey Him. Yep, there should be a fear factor and reverence factor here!

Mankind's biggest obstacle, that we all face, is coming to the realization that He is God and we are not. We have to face that fact several times in our lives. Returning to God and drawing close to Him, means that you are wanting to be *with* Him in every sense of the word; not just along for the ride... but *with* Him in total agreement with His plan for you and your family. That means loving Him and loving one another; finding ways to serve one another while representing Him and His Name. If that means turning your life around 180 degrees to return to Him... then do it. You will be glad you did.

We have been redeemed from the enslaving tyrant of sin-and-death in order to serve our Messiah, Yeshua. Today we are watching elected public servants, who are being paid with our money, becoming enslaving tyrants! It is the *power-of-sin* manifesting as the *sin-of-power* attacking our cities and enslaving the people. These tyrants are manifesting at all levels: federal, state, county, and city.

This didn't happen in a vacuum. This happened because Christians did not stay vigilant in being watchmen in all areas of our national life: government, schools, media, entertainment, business, religion, and families. Tyranny will always rise up when God's good men do nothing. Repentance always leads to Redemption. This need for repentance is much more than on the individual level. It ain't *Personal*, it's *National!*

This is a joint effort. Individually, if we serve Him, we will serve others as He did—willingly putting ourselves in the position of servant. Collectively, when we act as His permanent servants, is when we enjoy the true reality of freedom.

Psalms 31-33 are the suggested reading for today

Here is a taste

19 Oh, how great is Your goodness,
Which You have laid up for those who fear You,
Which You have prepared for those who trust in You
In the presence of the sons of men!
20 You shall hide them in the secret place of Your presence
From the plots of man;
You shall keep them secretly in a pavilion
From the strife of tongues.

Psalm 31:19-20

Abba… We know that we don't need to be afraid of You. We know that because of Yeshua's work on the cross that You have invited us to come boldly before Your throne of grace. We don't need to be afraid of You in one sense. Yet, in another sense, we need to be in awe of Who You are, What You have done, Why You have allowed us into Your Family and Kingdom. We apologize for not being diligent in guarding the gateways of our culture. We have been lazy, and apathetic while guarding our freedom.

When we consider, Who it is who loves us and made a way for us, it is almost more than we can take in. Help us to be Your servants, taking care of the gift of freedom that you have given to us, as Americans. Return to us; Restore us; Heal our land; Redeem us once again. Thank You, Abba for loving us the way You do.

Amen

Day 13

God Does Not Play Hide and Seek

Question: Do you even have a clue as to how special you are to God? Psalm 27 (remember… this is being read twice a day during these days of Elul) … speaks of God calling upon us to seek His face.

He summons everyone, because He summons each. He addresses each and every one of us separately, as though we were the only one He is speaking to. Yep, He is that awesome, and He thinks you're that special. His desire is for you. He seeks you out as well as you seeking Him. May it never be that you hear from your LORD: "Hey, I called but you refused to answer Me. I stretched out My hand, but you had no regard for it."

Think about this… if He commands us to seek Him… then He obligates Himself to be found by us. He will not play games of Hide and Seek with you. If you seek Him, He will be found by you. He is waiting for you under the Tree of Life. He will meet you, help you, save you, protect you, love you. He is the God of your salvation. All we have to do is turn in His direction and say, "Yes".

Hear, O Lord, when I cry with my voice! Have mercy also upon me, and answer me. [8] When You said, "Seek My face," My heart said to You, "Your face, Lord, I will seek." [9] Do not hide Your face from me; Do not turn Your servant away in anger; You have been my help; Do not leave me nor forsake me, O God of my salvation. [10] When my father and my mother forsake me, Then the Lord will take care of me.   Psalm 27:7-10

Psalms 34-36 are suggested reading for today

Here is a taste

[4] *I sought the Lord, and He heard me,*
And delivered me from all my fears.
[5] *They looked to Him and were radiant,*
And their faces were not ashamed.
[6] *This poor man cried out, and the Lord heard him,*
And saved him out of all his troubles. [7]
The angel of the Lord encamps all around those who fear Him,
And delivers them.

Psalm 34:4-7

Abba...

Everyone wants to feel special; as though we belong to someone or something outside of ourselves. We grow up in families and if we are lucky, we feel special to them. We have friends and we want to feel special to them. You made us that way... to have relationships. Relationships are important; and relationship with You is important! Forgive us for not nourishing our relationship with You. We can arise in the morning and not even acknowledge or thank You for another day of life. We can eat food and not thank You for providing it. Abba, forgive us for taking so many things for granted. You are very special.

Amen

Day 14

I am Guilty

Are we free from responsibility of Repentance? Scripture seems pretty clear that we shoulder responsibility of putting on the 'new man'... *Put on the new man which was created according to God, in true righteousness and holiness. Ephesians 4:24*

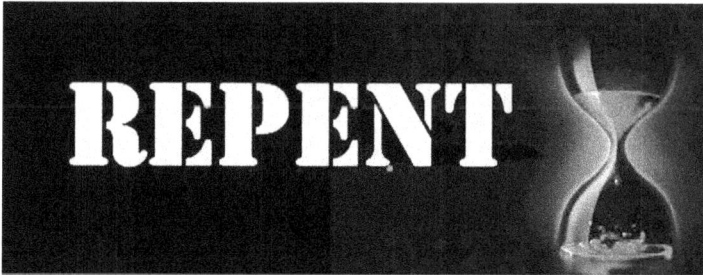

Here are some good things to take to the LORD in a prayer of repentance during this month; keeping in mind that repentance means changing one's mind about God and turning back to His ways.

Abba... I repent and turn from these things I am guilty of:

- For not walking in obedience to Your Word
- For prayerlessness, spiritual lethargy and irresponsibility
- For disunity in the family & home, and the Body of Messiah
- For accusing others
- For ungratefulness & pride
- For speaking idle words
- For unbelief, fear, and lack of faith
- For lack of vision, knowledge & passion to proclaim the Gospel

Psalms 37-40 are the suggested reading for today

Here is a taste

Mark the blameless man, and consider the upright, for the end of that man is peace. [38] But the transgressors will be destroyed together; the end of the wicked is to be cut off. [39] But the salvation of the righteous is from the Lord; He is their refuge in the time of distress. [40] The Lord will help them and deliver them; He will deliver them from the wicked, and save them, because they take refuge in Him.

Psalm 37:37

Abba...

We declare & proclaim, in the name of Yeshua, as we seek Your Face, that our Nation will become the Nation You have called us to be:

- *A nation of God's Righteousness, Peace & Blessing.*
- *A model nation to the world in education, employment & overall development*
- *A model nation for morality*
- *A model nation for justice, peace & harmony*
- *A model nation for overall health*
- *A model nation for good governance*
- *A model nation that is free of sex trafficking, prostitution, drugs, and abuse*
- *A model nation in ridding the challenges of racism, terrorism, anti-social & anti-national movements*
- *A Nation for God's glory*

In the Name of our Messiah, Yeshua

Day 15

Don't Forget Who You Are

Elul can also be read as an acronym for "Ani L'dodi Vdodi Li" (I am my beloved's, and my beloved is mine" from Song of Songs). These days of repentance are born out of love not fear. These are days of reflection are to draw us closer to the One who saved us out of this fallen world.

We all share the experience of having forgotten what you came into the room for! You step from one room to another and completely forget why you came in there. It helps to step back into the other room to remember. That is not dissimilar to the Children of Israel forgetting who they were and why God had brought them into the land of Promise.

Several times, in their Biblical history:

- They forgot who they were and why they were there.
- They forgot to consult the directions given them by Moses.
- They forgot there was only One God.
- They forgot they were to seek Him above all others.
- Leaders forgot to remember, and the people were left to wander after other gods.

There were three important positions of leadership in the Old Testament: Prophet, Priest and King. The Prophet always had access to the court of the King and didn't need an appointment. He would walk right in to see the king. God always sees that His messages are delivered. *Surely the Lord God does nothing, unless He reveals His secret to His servants, the prophets.* It is up to those in leadership to listen and do. Yeshua, of course, filled all three of those positions. Leadership under God's authority is a big responsibility, whether national or family. God always made sure that the Kings had a representative who had access to hear the Word of God.

> *⁷ This disaster came upon the nation of Israel because the people worshiped other gods, thus sinning against the Lord their God who had brought them safely out of their slavery in Egypt. ⁸ They had followed the evil customs of the nations which the Lord had cast out from before them. ⁹ The people of Israel had also secretly done many things that were wrong, and they had built altars to other gods throughout the land. ¹⁰ They had placed obelisks and idols at the top of every hill and under every green tree; ¹¹ and they had burned incense to the gods of the very nations which the Lord had cleared out of the land when Israel came in. So the people of Israel had done many evil things, and the Lord was very angry. ¹² Yes, they worshiped idols, despite the Lord's specific and repeated warnings.*
>
> *¹³ Again and again the Lord had sent prophets to warn both Israel and Judah to turn from their evil ways; he had warned them to obey his commandments which he had given to their ancestors through these prophets, ¹⁴ but Israel wouldn't listen. The people were as stubborn as their ancestors and refused to believe in the Lord their God. II Kings 17 NLT*

We, as a nation established by Covenant, are in danger of being described as, *forgetting who we are and why this nation was established!* We have been pulled back from the brink of catastrophic leadership in this country by God's mercy. But the solution is not political; it is spiritual. The politicians are not responsible for revival; God's people are! God will provide, as the people call for it, beginning with an attitude of repentance.

Let's shine a light on *Revival* vs. *Political* in the last century. Let's start in the middle of the century and work our way across the years. Let's talk Jubilee; a Biblical economic term for a cycle of 50 years. After a cycle of seven 7-year periods, the 50th year is called a Jubilee. Among other things, during a Jubilee year, land was returned to its proper owner and debts were cancelled. It was like hitting the reset button.

It was in 1967, *after* the Six-Day-War, that things started heating up in *Revival* mode. The restoration of Jerusalem to the Jewish people marked the fulfillment of Yeshua's prophecy recorded in **Luke 21:24: "Jerusalem will be trampled on by the Gentiles until the times of the Gentiles are fulfilled."** One of the largest revivals in history began that year… 1967; the year of Jubilee!

That year - 1967 and that event - Jerusalem coming back into the hands of the Jewish people- half-way through the year, sparked the latest Great Revival.

So, what happened?

- Jewish Messianic Congregations began to be established; Jews realized they could believe in Jesus and be Jewish.
- The Jesus Movement picked up speed; many young people came to believe in Jesus.
- The Charismatic movement was a God-send as the Holy Spirit was being poured out across the land.

In Israel, the Tourist trade was birthed, as both Jews and Christians went to visit the land that had been off limits. Israel exploded in technology, military defense systems, agriculture, medicine, technology, oil/gas was discovered off their shores, etc. That was (just) over 50 years ago and the last Jubilee.

The hordes of hell didn't welcome any of these movements and got busy with its counter-moves: sexual perversion and human trafficking, drug cartels, free love, rebellion, corruption, bombings of innocent people, and Middle East wars. Those 50 years took up the majority of our life's time.

The previous Jubilee year was 1917, when the Balfour Declaration was issued by the British government announcing support for a homeland for the Jewish people. (Think of the counter-moves and wars that followed that statement!)

The most recent Jubilee year happened in 2017 - (they happen every 50 years). The key event of 2017 was the United States recognizing Jerusalem as the capital of Israel. The newly elected President of the United States declared he would move the Embassy, like many other presidents said they would. But President Trump actually did it!

Congress approved the recognition of Jerusalem as the capital of Israel on June 5, 2017; the 50th anniversary of Jerusalem being returned to the Jews. On May 14, 2018 the American Embassy opened in Jerusalem, during the year of Jubilee; and Israel's 70th anniversary of their independence.

The hordes of hell didn't like this political move either. The response from the evil one has been non-stop. We are witnessing the 24/7 attempted overthrow of the government of the United States of America; directed by Satan; allowed by Heaven; result pending Repentance.

This coup is beyond the bounds and scope of politics. The demonic realm is being forced to expose itself. If this is going to end well, for America, then Repentance and Returning to God is the answer. It is time for the Church to willingly expose itself, repenting for the lack willingness to be involved at the gates of our culture.

Let's follow the path of Repentance and Consolation, during these days of Elul, to the end and see where it leads us. We won't be sorry. If we do follow the path, we are just being obedient to His Word. He is still waiting for us... under the Tree of Life... to meet with Him and talk with Him in the cool of the day. These little talks can make a BIG Difference.

Psalms 40-42 are suggested reading for today

Here is a taste

Psalm 40:3 He has put a new song in my mouth, even praise to our God; many will see it, and fear, and will trust in the Lord.

Abba... We are so in need of Revival, or a movement of Your Spirit, or an Awakening. We have been sleepy or lethargic or apathetic or lazy or slothful with the things of the Spirit. Forgive us for taking our eyes off of the prize and lead us to Repentance. I don't know who we thought would be responsible to take the Gospel to the nations and make disciples of them. I guess we thought 'George' would do it. Abba, awaken Your church and revive our purpose within us. We need and want to take a giant step forward toward Your Kingdom. Help us recover: the government, the schools, the media, the arts/entertainment industry, the business community, and the Church. Lord, rescue our children and our grandchildren from the onslaught of the enemy of our souls. Amen

Day 16

Revival Involves Recovery of Truth

Is there a desire for Revival in our lifetime? Do you desire to see people coming to the LORD in droves as it happened in the late 60's and 70's? (Hmmmm… after Jerusalem came back into the hands of the rightful owner… at the last Jubilee!)

One prayer that every committed Believer should be praying is that God would send revival to our country and the world in this generation. As Isaiah reminds us, *"the Lord's hand is not so short that it cannot save; neither is His ear so dull that it cannot hear" Isa 59:1*

What applies nationally to our need for revival also applies personally to you. Luke tells us that, *the Son of Man has come to seek and to save that which was lost (19:10).* If you feel lost or in despair, then you are a candidate for His grace.

This is where we are 'important gears' in the machinery of how things work. As we join in Teshuva, (turning back to God's grace) during this time of Repentance - these 40 days prior to – Yom Kippur… we are participating in the process.

We should be asking God for a Revival, even a Reformation, that will shake our nation and shake the world... causing the blinders to come off the eyes of loved ones, including our Jewish brothers and sisters. The funny thing is, it will happen whether we participate or not, because somewhere people are repenting. But it would be good to participate.

True Reformation is not a superficial, emotional response resulting in a temporary experience. It produces long term fruit that is called *Love for God* and *Love for one another*.

Revival always involves a recovery of biblical truth. Reconciliation to a Holy God is always good for a nation. We have lived long enough to have seen many Jewish people coming to Messiah... in droves... after all of Jerusalem came back into Israel's hands. We have seen the days of the Charismatic Movement. And we have seen the Jesus Movement among hippies. These were all movements of grace that exploded across the face of the earth.

This revival of the 60's - 70's was during another time of division and hatred and unrest and war... another ugly time in our country's history. Hmmm... sounds kind of like today! We need that kind of grace poured out again. But we need to cry out for it... and yes it will be messy... because it goes with the territory.

Psalms 43-45 are the suggested reading for today

Here is a taste

[13] The bride, a princess, waits within her chamber, robed in beautiful clothing woven with gold. [14] Lovely she is, led beside her maids of honor to the king! [15] What a joyful, glad procession as they enter in the palace gates! [16] "Your sons will some day be kings like their father. They shall sit on thrones around the world!

[17] "I will cause your name to be honored in all generations; the nations of the earth will praise you forever."

Psalm 45:13-17 TLB

Abba,

Send Your Holy Spirit amongst us again and lead us to Your throne of grace. We are a confused people and in need of Your Mercy and Grace for this generation. Draw us together as Your people. We ask for a time of Visitation from Your Spirit to turn our faces toward You once again.

We cry out to You to restore our hearts, so that we may love and honor You and love one another in the way that You have directed. Fill our lamps with fresh oil. Send Revival our way.

Help us to understand 2 Chronicles 7:14 in a new way... as we humble ourselves before You and watch You heal our land. Help us and our loved ones to discover and recover the Truth in Your Word.

In the Name of our Messiah, Yeshua

Day 17

Great Revivals Have Personality

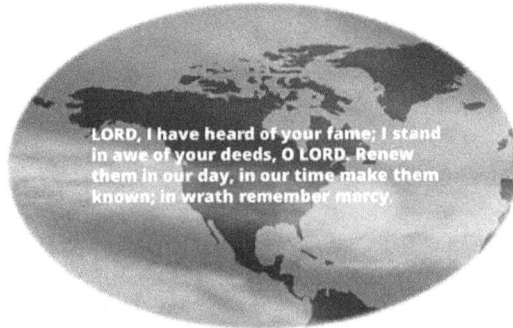

LORD, I have heard of your fame; I stand in awe of your deeds, O LORD. Renew them in our day, in our time make them known; in wrath remember mercy.

We can all agree that our land is in need of Revival. It only comes through Repentance and/or a sovereign act on His part. We turn our hearts toward the LORD… seeking His face and favor. Consider this list of genuine revivals that have taken place in this country as a result of Repentance.

- The Great Awakening, 1734-43.
- The Second Great Awakening, 1800-1840
- The Businessmen's Revival of 1857-1858.
- The Civil War Revival, 1861-1865.
- The Urban Revivals, 1875-1885
- The Revivals of 1905-1906.
- The Azusa Street Revival, 1906.
- The Post-World War II Awakening. After World War II, in 1947 and 1948
- The Charismatic Renewal and Jesus Movement. During the late 1960s and early 1970s

- The Asbury Revival 1970
- The Mid-1990s Revivals.
- The Promise Keepers Revival, the most publicized of the mid-1990s Revivals, began in 1991 when 4,200 men descended on the University of Colorado to be challenged to live up to their faith.

Revivals have personality! Each one signs its signature for history to remember it by. If we look at three revivals over the last three centuries, we could identify them by the 'signature' they left.

- In 1740 - youth led the way
- In 1857 - businessmen and prayer took center stage
- In 1906 - Azusa Street revival was distinctly interracial

God loves variety and seldom does the same thing twice in the same way. Variety yes, but all share common themes. We can ask, "What do revivals and awakenings have in common when their story is told?"

1. **TIMING:** Revivals are a response to prayer in times of need. They don't just pop up but will emerge during times of spiritual and moral decline. God responds to His peoples' prayers

2. **THE WORD:** The preaching or reading of God›s Word brings deep conviction and desire for Yeshua.

3. **THE HOLY SPIRIT:** The Holy Spirit will come and teach and take people to a spiritual depth they could not achieve on their own.

4. **CONVICTION:** The Holy Spirit will convict people of sin.

5. **GLORY FOR GOD**: God receives praise, honor, and glory for bringing revival.

6. **RESET**: Spiritual fruit will be the result of revival. People are put back in their right minds... even as the demoniac was when Yeshua cast out the legion of demons. Society experiences a reform of morals. Justice and Righteousness will patrol the cities and walk the streets as more and more people come to the LORD.

Revival always leads to new levels of PRAISE and WORSHIP. Let's face it... that is why we are here... to praise and worship God... not us! As the days get more and more crazy, let's remember what we are supposed to be doing.

Psalms 46-48 are the suggested reading for today

Here is a taste

¹ God is our refuge and strength, always ready to help in times of trouble.
² So we will not fear when earthquakes come and the mountains crumble into the sea.
³ Let the oceans roar and foam. Let the mountains tremble as the waters surge!

Psalm 46:1

Abba… the seas are raging, the storms are devastating, the fires are consuming, the riots are destroying our land. Use these troubles to turn us to You, and call out to You to help us, and to heal us, and bring us to You. Help us help one another with love and compassion.

Amen

Day 18

An Act of Love!

God Loves You *Infinitely*.

During this time of turning to our faces toward God and not away from Him... we discover during this month of Elul - (Harvest, Repentance, and Consolation) that He loves us a great deal! In fact, God's Word says, what the greatest act of love is: *"Greater love has no one than this, that one lay down his life for his friends." John 15:13*

O, the depth of the riches of the wisdom and knowledge of God! How unsearchable His judgments, and untraceable His ways! Romans 11:33

His sacrifice is even more monumental and loving when we consider that He bore our sins in his body on the cross. Undoubtedly, Yeshua indeed performed the greatest act of love. It is not only what He did for us... it's Who He is! He is God and He loved us so much that He came in a body prepared for Him to offer Himself once-and-for-all. Never again would a blood sacrifice for sin be required. His redemption of us is complete.

We celebrate that in the guarding of His appointed times. In hearing and doing, we will never forget:

It is Yeshua who we come to	**John 1:12**
It is Yeshua who cleanses us from sin	**I John 1:7**
It is Yeshua who reveals grace and truth	**John 1:17**
It is Yeshua who is called God	**Hebrews 1:8**
It is Yeshua who is the first and last	**Revelation 1:17**
It is Yeshua who gives eternal life	**John 10:28**
It is Yeshua who draws people to Himself	**John 12:32**
It is Yeshua who will manifest Himself to us	**John 14:21**
It is Yeshua who opens our minds to understand the Scriptures	**Luke 24:45**

Psalms 49-51 are the suggested reading for today

Here is a taste

What I want from you is your true thanks;
I want your promises fulfilled.
I want you to trust Me in your times of trouble,
so I can rescue you and you can give Me glory.
Psalm 50:14-15 TLB

Abba,

Help us to be thankful for what Yeshua has done for us. Help us to be committed to Your Body of Believers, to our families, our extended families, to our friends.

Lord, these are difficult days and we all desire to find You in the midst of them. We desire to love You and to love one another; that is what we say. Help our words to be full of meaning, for this is what Your Torah is all about. Help us to release Your Kingdom here and now. Help us to be encouragers of one another and to demonstrate Yeshua's love to others.

We openly declare now that Revival is in the Land of the United States of America. The difficult days that are upon millions of Americans will be for good and will draw us together as Your people turning back to You… for help and consolation. Teach us to trust and believe and love and help.

In the Name of our Messiah

Day 19

Don't Squander Your Authority

In the past few years, we have seen storms, flood, winds, fires and now, riots have brought devastation across the United States. Are we, as God's people, just supposed to sit by watching this happen? Did Yeshua not say to the storm, "Peace, be still!"?

As we think of our fellow Americans, in the wake of the riots and devastating aftermath in large cities all across the land, what kind of prayers should we be praying? Many governors and mayors are becoming self-realized demigods wielding power over people they have been elected to serve.

Prayers that express, "Lord, bless them and keep them safe"; or "Lord, help them", perhaps should be more forceful! Please remember that prayer is not asking a reluctant God to do something. Prayer is about coming into agreement with God and others, and petitioning God to act according to His Will.

There are things that He has given you authority over. Yeshua said, *"Behold, I give you the authority to trample on serpents and scorpions, and over all the power of the enemy, and nothing shall by any means hurt you." Luke 10:19.* This bears witness that Yeshua gave this kind of authority to His disciples. Authority such as this is available to those who have clean hands and pure hearts and whose face is turned toward God, not away from Him.

Yeshua is your best friend as well as King of Israel. Together, you can face whatever comes up during the day: pleasures, hardships, disappointments, adventures. Bring it on… because nothing is wasted when shared with Him. He is the One who brings beauty out of ashes. He's waiting for you to join Him and use the authority He has given to you. Remember, the nations are His inheritance! Don't squander your authority, or take His authority lightly.

Go and talk to Him about American cities under siege!

Psalms 52-54 are the suggested reading for today

Here is a taste

⁴ But God is my helper. He is a friend of mine!...
⁶ Gladly I bring my sacrifices to you;
I will praise your name, O Lord, for it is good.
⁷ God has rescued me from all my trouble,
and triumphed over my enemies.

Psalm 54: 4-7 TLB

Abba…

We come before You, seeking Your face and asking You to heal our land. We have stood by watching sections of our cities be destroyed. We wonder why some governors and mayors do nothing. We wonder how the idea of no police and no national guard being allowed to do their jobs is even possible, let alone an American thing to do.

Then we realize that this is the result of not being vigilant about our country. We have not taken our place as watchmen on the wall. We have not taken authority over the demonic forces that would destroy our country, our institutions, our government and our families. Father, forgive us and help us to return to You. Turn our apathy into enthusiasm for Justice, Righteousness, and Mercy.

Amen

Day 20

Walking in Agreement with God

"Our deepest fear is not that we are inadequate. Our deepest fear is that we are powerful beyond measure. We ask ourselves, Who am I to be brilliant, gorgeous, talented, fabulous? Actually, who are you not to be? We were born to make manifest the glory of God that is within us. And as we let our light shine, we unconsciously give other people permission to do the same." (M. Williamson)

Now, you can agree with that statement or not. I first heard it in a movie-called... **Akeela and the Bee**... about the National Spelling Bee that occurs in Washington D.C. each year. It is a true story of a little girl from LA who worked very hard... studying all year to win a spot at the National Finals.

She felt betrayed by her coach, one day, when he handed her a box of a thousand words to learn. At first, she was not able to understand what had happened. Feeling very abandoned and alone, her friend and coach seemed to turn away from her when she needed him the most.

She finally was able to learn the lesson her coach was trying to teach her. She couldn't do it alone. She needed to lean on the people in her community, people of the streets of LA, to help her learn the lessons the words had to teach her. Yes, the words *themselves* had lessons to teach her. She learned… not just how to spell them i.e. *form* but also the meaning and origin i.e. *function*. These words became her friends.

God's Word has lessons to teach us as well. But we have to read them… and practice them over and over. These lessons are our friends… if we allow them to be. We are born to make manifest the glory of God, but we won't and can't do it without learning the lessons His Word has to offer.

Like this one: Walking in **agreement** with God is a good goal and can be likened to walking in **harmony** with a friend. Walking in agreement with a friend makes the walk easier; the harmony sound sweeter. It identifies the melody and defines the purpose of the relationship. However, when harmony between people is broken, it is as though a record has obtained a big scratch. The song they share loses its beauty and can't get beyond the scratch. That is sad. The remedy is repentance and apology. The season of opportunity is now. This season of teshuva (returning) is like a *big scratch remover*. That is what the month of Elul has to offer: returning to Him and receiving His Consolation. This is Bride Prep time, Beloved. Let's not miss the opportunity.

a·gree·ment .... noun

> harmony or accordance in opinion or feeling; a position or result of agreeing.

har·mo·ny .... noun

> the combination of simultaneously sounded musical notes to produce chords and chord progressions having a pleasing effect.

Psalms 55-57 are the suggested reading for today

Here is a taste

Be merciful to me, O God, be merciful to me! For my soul trusts in You;
And in the shadow of Your wings I will make my refuge, Until these calamities have
passed by. ² I will cry out to God Most High, To God who performs all things for me.
³ He shall send from heaven and save me;
He reproaches the one who would swallow me up. Selah

Psalm 57: 1-3

Abba...

As believers and Your children, we desire to walk in harmony with You. Our life-paths can take some interesting turns and tumbles. But if we are walking in harmony with You and in agreement with Your Word, what a wonderful walk or hike or trek it will be. We can feel it in the center of our very being when we are walking in agreement with You. You speak to us in such gentle tones, and affirming ways. Oh, that we would respond quickly to You and when we mess up, may we be quick to seek Your forgiveness, because You forgive and restore. Help us to treat others that way as well.

We have so many things to learn from You and from one another. How we learn is through the gift of words. Your Word became flesh and dwelt among us and taught us about You. May we use our words to help those around us learn about Your Word.

Amen

*Let's remember.... **there is no condemnation to those who are in Christ Jesus.***

Day 21

God Will Remember for Us!

From Leviticus 26… A very important verse shows a very special and important fact about God that is covered by one of those 'small' words. The word is "FOR".

Look at this:

God remains faithful because He is God

⁴⁴ Yet for all that, when they are in the land of their enemies, I will not cast them away, nor shall I abhor them, to utterly destroy them and break My covenant with them; for I *am* the LORD their God.

⁴⁵ But for their sake I will remember the covenant of their ancestors, whom I brought out of the land of Egypt in the sight of the nations, that I might be their God: I *am* the LORD.' "

This Chapter was a reminder that God's people have a Covenant with Him. Even though God's people will forget the Covenant and will pay dearly for their forgetfulness, ultimately, God is the One who will remember for them the Covenant. **'But I will remember *for* them the covenant with their ancestors…'**

Read that again slowly… He will remember the Covenant **for** them (and you).

God is always faithful to His Covenant. Do you remember when He made the Covenant with Abraham? He put him into a deep sleep and walked through the animal pieces of spilled blood Himself. He committed to the Covenant then - for both parties! God initiated this Covenant, and then they began a new relationship with one another. This

Covenant would continue through his son, and his son's son, and his son's son's sons! (Think about it!) God and Abraham became Covenant Friends.

Having a Covenant with God, who is faithful, has got to be the most secure possession a person has. No wonder that Yeshua asked, *"When the Son of Man returns will He find faithfulness on the earth?"*

We need to be about our Father's business here in these days that are looking more and more like the end of days. Returning to Him, and being the best representative of Him that we can be to those in our circle of influence, should be our top priority. Yeshua has called us His friends.

No longer do I call you servants, for a servant does not know what his master is doing; but I have called you friends, for all things that I heard from My Father I have made known to you. John 15:15

Yeshua is our Covenant Friend!

No wonder we want to stay close to and draw near to our God. No wonder this month of Elul is so important! We have a Covenant with Him to draw from, and call on. Tests and trials will come. It is part of living in a fallen world. We have the privilege and honor of having the Holy Spirit dwelling in us because He desires to do so. It is the Spirit of the Living God Who will pass the test for us, if we will but allow Him to do so. (think about it!) It is an open book test; we can ask the teacher any question.

Think of all the generations that have gone by, passed by, since the days of Abraham; all the blood that was spilled on the altars of the Israelites: until the last sacrifice for sin was made by God Himself. We are the beneficiaries of that sacrifice! *Colossians 2:13,14 ………. having wiped out the handwriting of requirements that was against us……. And He has taken it out of the way, having nailed it to the cross.*

Psalms 58-60 is the suggested reading for today

Here is a taste

But I will sing of Your power;
Yes, I will sing aloud of Your mercy in the morning;
For You have been my defense
And refuge in the day of my trouble.
[17] To You, O my Strength, I will sing praises;
For God is my defense,
My God of mercy.

Psalm 59: 16-17

Abba...

What a beautiful concept. You are my Covenant Friend! We, who know little of what the word, 'Covenant' even means, are the beneficiary of it! You made it, You kept it, You caused it to prevail. And because You did all those things, we (ignorant or not) reap the benefits of the Covenant. Thank You, Abba, for Your faithfulness to us. We Western-Culture-people have so much to learn about the way Your Kingdom operates... all built on Covenant. Oh, that we would dare to take the time to learn of it. We would demand more from our shepherds and we would give more to the sheep. Thank You for what You have accomplished for us through the Covenant we have with You. Amen

Day 22

America ~ God's Idea

9/11 on our yearly calendars is like a photo album in everyone's memory. We know where we were, who we were with, and how we felt as we all watched, with shock and awe, what was happening in our country.

As I have been reading the Psalms that are attached to these days of Elul, I wonder what was going on with David. He, too, had so many enemies who were out to get him, kill him, harm him, and hate him. We live in a world like that. The enemy knows his time is short and is seeking whom he may devour. He hates us. He doesn't play by any rules or obey any laws.

While the protests and riots continue their shaking and testing of our faith... let's remain steadfast and grounded in His Word. It will never let us down. May we never forget the God of our salvation... and the purpose of this land He has granted to us... and the destiny of the United States and the American people.

I found this quote from a paper, when googling 'American Destiny': *"If there be a destiny, it is of no avail for us unless we work with it. The ways of Providence will be of no advantage to us unless we proceed in the same direction. If we perceive a destiny in America, if we believe that Providence has been the guide, our own success, our own salvation require that we should act and serve in harmony and obedience."* Calvin Coolidge

Hmmmm… There is that word *harmony* again. This quote is really talking about the Covenant that we have with God. This country, America, was God's idea… from the get-go. This was to be a landing spot for the gathering of all the Tribes of Israel. Well, 200 plus years later, here we are; a nation deeply divided being tossed about in the winds and storms and fires all around. We need to proceed in the same direction as *Providence* would have us go: pulling together, joining together, supporting one another. We are to be in complete agreement *with* God, (עם 'eem' *agreement in purpose*) as He takes us into His future Kingdom right here on earth.

It is good to know that we have a Rock to go to, to stand on, to run to and to be sheltered by… in the storms and trials of this life.

Psalms 61-63 is the suggested reading for today

Here is a taste

⁵ Let all that I am wait quietly before God, for my hope is in him.
⁶ He alone is my rock and my salvation, my fortress where I will not be shaken.
⁷ My victory and honor come from God alone. He is my refuge, a rock where no enemy can reach me. ⁸ O my people, trust in him at all times. Pour out your heart to him, for God is our refuge.

Psalm 62:5-8

Abba… What a shocking and tragic memory that day was for all of us. It was a beautiful day in late summer. The United States was going about its business, and just like that… everything changed. Oh, God… how long does it have to take to come back to You? How long will it take for us to cry out to You? We started; we hung out our flags; we opened up our churches and they were filled. But after a few months we went back to our way doing things… we went to war… again!

LORD, here we are twenty years later and what do we look like? We are no longer united. We are divided: left and right; Socialists and Patriots; masked and unmasked. The American flag is burned and stomped. The media lies to us. The police are defunded and disrespected and attacked. Major cities have been burned and looted. The prisons are being emptied. Your people are armed, and learning how and when to handle a gun. The capital buildings have been defaced and graffitied. Governors and Mayors are not acting like elected officials, but tyrants. Small businesses are closed, restaurants are half-full. The schools are closed. Universities won't allow conservative speakers on their campus; many universities won't allow students on campus. Memorial statues are being torn down. The Founding Fathers are accused of being men of ill repute and suspect.

All of this because of an unseen enemy. Oh, we blame an unseen virus… but LORD, You know the unseen enemy is the enemy of our soul. We can't fix this. Without Your help and intervention, we will lose this generation to the enemy. Abba, help us. We plead the blood of Yeshua over our beloved county. Heal our land, save Your people and pull up the tares in this harvest. Forgive us. Turn Your face toward us again, for our children and our grandchildren. Bind the powers and principalities that have been loosed on us.

Thank You for not forgetting the Covenant that this country has with You. We will wait for it! We call on You to heal our land and to hear our cries. We have no where to turn, but to You. Hear and Heal us. We Praise You for the Great things You have done. May the earth soon hear Your voice. May we all soon rejoice as we give You Glory for the Covenant that You have made with us and are upholding in spite of us. Amen

Day 23

Part 1 ~ Yeshua's Forty Days

What about Yeshua? Is there any indication of what He did during His 40 days in the Wilderness? If we understand these Hebrew hints that help-us-connect-the-dots, then yes, we can recognize what He did during that time of isolation.

Mark and Luke and Matthew let us know what happened...

Yeshua was baptized by John the Baptist and the Spirit descended out of heaven and **sent Him out into the wilderness for 40 days.** Mark says, *The Spirit immediately drove him out into the wilderness. ESV* He was not alone however; Satan, wild beasts (demons) were there too, and angels ministered to Him during this period. If the Spirit drove Him.... then He was "dropped off" at the Mountain of God... in the Wilderness of Mt. Sinai. That is the Wilderness in the Bible!

Yeshua was not there to repent and come close to God. He was fully God and fully man after all! The Holy Spirit had just descended on Him after His baptism saying, *"This is My Beloved Son in Whom I Am well pleased."*

The Jubilee Year would begin soon after these 40 days. This Jubilee Year is the one where the plan of salvation would be laid out. Yeshua would announce it at Yom Kippur. Satan tried cutting a deal with Yeshua and presented his proposal in 3 options.

1. Turn the stones to bread. (do a miracle…prove it) *"No! For the Scriptures tell us that bread won't feed men's souls: obedience to every word of God is what we need." TLB*

2. All the kingdoms of the world were offered to Yeshua provided that He would worship the devil. *"Get out of here, Satan," Jesus told him. "The Scriptures say, 'Worship only the Lord God. Obey only him.'" TLB*

3. Yeshua was taken to Jerusalem and told to throw Himself down. (surely you won't die) *"It also says not to put the Lord your God to a foolish test!" TLB*

The WORD OF GOD used only the *Word of God* in this meeting with Satan and his demons. Satan was challenging Yeshua - tempting Him - now that his human nature was hungry. But He only responded with what had been written.

15 This High Priest of ours understands our weaknesses since he had the same temptations we do, though he never once gave way to them and sinned. Hebrews 4:1 MSG

Those must have been days of anguish for Yeshua's humanity. However, they were essential in establishing the Kingdom in all Righteousness as He told John at His baptism.

15 But be holy now in everything you do, just as the Lord is holy, who invited you to be his child. 16 He himself has said, "You must be holy, for I am holy." I Peter 1:15-16 TLB

Psalms 64-66 are the suggested reading for today

Here is a taste

He formed the mountains by his mighty strength. 7 He quiets the raging oceans and all the world's clamor. 8 In the farthest corners of the earth the glorious acts of God shall startle everyone. The dawn and sunset shout for joy! 9 He waters the earth to make it fertile. The rivers of God will not run dry! He prepares the earth for his people and sends them rich harvests of grain.

Psalm 65:6 TLB

Abba…

Your meeting with Satan in the Wilderness was brilliant! What can we learn from that?

- *Obedience is important;*
- *Worship only God,*
- *Don't put God to a foolish test.*

God forgive us for not obeying You, not worshiping You, and for all the times we have tested You and acted foolishly in doing so. LORD, prepare our hearts, even as You are preparing the earth for the great harvest of souls. Amen

Day 24

Part 2 ~ Yeshua's Forty Days

It was during these days in the Wilderness where the battle for you began. The battle plan was being mapped out as Yeshua was at the Mountain of God on Mt. Sinai in what is now Saudi Arabia. His ministry in the Galilee was about to begin. As Moses spent 40 days and nights on the mountain with God… so did Yeshua spend 40 days and nights there.

Think about this: While Moses was on the Mountain with God, God was teaching Moses about the Tabernacle and how to build it and what would be in it and what it would look like so that He could live among His People. Here, Yeshua was on the Mountain with Satan and the demons, being tested in His flesh. Perhaps the objectives of His ministry were being drafted or defined or described so that all righteousness would be fulfilled in putting down the rebellion that happened in the Garden. Perhaps it was like listing Teaching Objectives in a Lesson Plan.

Let's just say that it was. Yeshua's Lesson Plan could have looked something like this:

GOALS

1. Read from the book of Isaiah in the synagogue announcing the Year of Jubilee.

Isaiah 61: 1"The Spirit of the Lord God is upon Me, Because the Lord has anointed Me To preach good tidings to the poor; He has sent Me to heal the brokenhearted, To proclaim liberty to the captives, And the opening of the prison to those who are bound; 2 To proclaim the acceptable year of the Lord.

Announce the year of Jubilee....

- The debt for sin is going to be cancelled and paid for.
- The captives are to be freed from the law of sin and death.
- Those bound by demonic forces are going to be set free.
- Those bound by sickness will be healed... for this is the acceptable year (Jubilee Year of the LORD) Wait for it!

2. Plan the journey through the Land: picking up 12 Disciples along the route; looking for at least 10 men who would believe what I Am about to do; going up to Jerusalem as the Passover Lamb; paying the price for the sins of all mankind.

3. Redemption for mankind to be completed at Passover. My blood from Heaven will be the last blood required to be spilled for the sins of man. I will pay the price Myself.

   a. ***God will provide Himself the lamb for the burnt offering. Gen18***

   b. ***I will remember the Covenant for them... Lev. 26***

OBJECTIVES:

My People will know that:

- I AM announcing the Year of Jubilee.... (as per Isaiah 61)
- I AM the Messiah
- I AM the One sent from Heaven
- I came from the Tribe of Judah and therefore am the Son of David
- I came in a body prepared to be the last sacrifice for sin... the Lamb slain from the foundation of the world
- My blood, which comes from heaven, will be the only acceptable blood for the remission of sins from now on
- I and My Father are One
- I have come to be the Passover Lamb offered up by the Gentiles and the Jews
- I willingly lay down My life; no one takes it from Me
- I and My Father will not leave nor forsake My people
- I will die on a tree by Roman hands but will be raised to life after three days
- Upon My return to heaven, I will send the Holy Spirit to once again dwell in the hearts of men
- I will build My House of living stones, who will be jointly fit together

- I will expect My people to guard My Commands to love Me and to love one another.

- I will come again at the end of the ages to dwell with them and they will rule with Me

---

Yes, gentle reader… this is an imaginative 'look inside' what could have happened at Mt. Sinai in Arabia at the time of Yeshua's trip to the wilderness for 40 days. Because when these days were done, His ministry got underway and He met all those Goals and Objectives. He read, what today is, Isaiah 61: verse 1 and half of verse 2. He then stopped, sat down and said, ***"Today this Scripture is fulfilled in your hearing."*** The rest of verse 2 (and beyond) He is saving for the next time He comes. (Wait for it!) I'll let you look that up. The time to seek Him is now. The good news of His first coming is still available to all.

Psalms 67-69 are the suggested reading for today

Here is a taste

O God, in mercy bless us; let your face beam with joy as you look down at us.
² Send us around the world with the news of your saving power and your eternal plan for all mankind. ³ How everyone throughout the earth will praise the Lord! ⁴ How glad the nations will be, singing for joy because you are their King and will give true justice to their people.

Psalm 67:1

Abba…

You are so organized! Your plans are established and have been since the beginning of creation. Thank You for letting us see what did. Your acts were not random, neither did you wonder what was going to happen on any given day. Your Plan is good, Your way is sure, Your mercy endures forever. You are Truth!

Amen

Day 25

Keep the Light On

"You are the light of the world. A city that is set on a hill cannot be hidden.
[15] Nor do they light a lamp and put it under a basket, but on a lampstand, and it gives
light to all who are in the house. [16] Let your light so shine before men, that they may
see your good works and glorify your Father in heaven. Matthew 5:14-16

These are the words spoken by Yeshua to the people of Israel who were following Him after the start of His ministry in the Galilee… two thousand years ago. Thirty-five-hundred years ago, the Israelites were commanded to keep a flame burning on the altar in the Tabernacle as a symbol of His Presence among them. What about today?

In synagogues, wherever they are, you will find an 'eternal flame' burning near the Ark that holds the Torah Scroll. The rabbis teach that it is the responsibility of each individual to keep a light alive in their hearts. Israelis understand their responsibility to be a light to the world representing the God of Abraham, Isaac and Jacob.

In 'keeping the light on' for the world to see, Israel… a tiny country of 7 million Jews, is one of the first responders to countries beyond their borders in times of emergencies. Whether earthquakes in Haiti, Japan, and Kashmir; deadly storms in America, Philippines, Congo, Indonesia just to name a few, Israel will be on the scene helping. It doesn't matter where… Israeli humanitarian aid is there to help alleviate suffering. Their help knows no boundaries. This is their response to many nations, who officially vote against them in the UN: suit up, show up, stand up for those in need.

Over the last 26 years, Israel has sent out 15 aid missions to countries struck by natural disasters. Immediately upon arriving in these countries, IDF doctors set up field hospitals. Often, they are the first to arrive on scene. Yep, guess you could say that Israel is keeping the light on for you. They are doing good to those who persecute them. When someone needs help, they don't turn away from them, they run toward them.

Psalms 70-72 are the suggested reading for today

Here is a taste

Let all those who seek You rejoice and be glad in You;
And let those who love Your salvation say continually,
"Let God be magnified!"

Psalm 70:4

Abba….

Thank You for the Israelis who guard Your precepts to help those in need. May Your Light shine upon them so that they see the Light of the Messiah Yeshua just waiting for them to return to Him. May they soon say, "Blessed is He Who comes in the Name of Yahuah."

Amen

Day 26

Don't Hold Your Own Hand

Life can sometimes be difficult, even harsh. Sometimes, we can feel alone, discouraged or feel like we are carrying the weight of the world on our shoulders. If you ever feel like that then it is time to realize what a Helper we have in Yeshua. You were never meant to carry that kind of weight. Your shoulders are too fragile.

Yeshua said, ***"My yoke is easy and my burden is light."*** That is why He wants us to walk with Him… (even that is wrong!) The right thing to say is, He wants to walk with us! The yoke He has for you will be a perfect fit for you… and Him together.

When we choose to walk alone, forgetting Him or leaving Him behind, is when our way gets difficult. Don't kick Him to the curb and wander off by yourself. If you have, this is the perfect time to return to Him. That is what this month is all about - returning to Him! He is waiting with open arms for all the prodigals to come home. He is even standing on the edge of the road searching for them!

To think that we can worship Him as King of Kings, while walking hand in hand with Him, is a wonderful thought. As you walk out this day with Him, think of relating to Him as:

- creature to Creator
- sheep to Shepherd
- subject to King
- clay to Potter
- child to Father

Keep Him close. Hold His hand. It is a perfect fit. And in the strength of it you will find strength. It is much better than holding your own hand! Like the two-year old at the corner who refused his mother's hand saying instead, "me hold me own hand!" That seldom works.

Psalms 73-75 are the suggested reading for today

Here is a taste

But even so, you love me! You are holding my right hand!
²⁴ You will keep on guiding me all my life with your wisdom
and counsel, and afterwards receive me into the glories of heaven!
²⁵ Whom have I in heaven but you?
And I desire no one on earth as much as you!

Psalm 73:23

Abba…

How sweet to think that we can walk with You. Sweeter still to think that You want to walk with us! What a comfort to know that we can walk with You and even reach out for Your hand to hold. When we get quiet enough, we can tell You anything, ask any question, and then we can hear You answer us. Yeshua, Thank You for accepting us into Your Kingdom and the help that You offer to Your people. What a wonderful thought that You are only a whisper away.

Amen

Day 27

Advice From an Old Farmer

Old Farmer's Advice
by former Judge and Texas State Legislator Roy English

Your fences need to be horse-high, pig-tight and bull-strong.
Keep skunks and bankers at a distance.
Life is simpler when you plow around the stump.
Words that soak into your ears are whispered.....not yelled.
Meanness don't just happen overnight.
Keep tellin' yourself your better than the rest, soon you'll be your only fan.
Forgive your enemies; it messes up their heads.
Do not corner something that you know is meaner than you.
It don't take a very big person to carry a grudge.
When you wallow with pigs, expect to get dirty.
The best sermons are lived, not preached.

Most of the stuff people worry about, ain't never gonna happen anyway.
Don't judge folks by their relatives.
Remember that silence is sometimes the best answer.
Live a good and honorable life, then when you get older and think back,
you'll enjoy it a second time.
Money doesn't make a person smarter, nicer or better in any way.
The biggest troublemaker you'll probably ever have to deal with, watches you
from the mirror every mornin'.
Always drink upstream from the herd.
Good judgment comes from experience, and a lotta that comes from bad judgment.
If you get to thinkin' you're a person of some influence,
try orderin' somebody else's dog around.
Live simply, love generously, care deeply, speak kindly, and leave the rest to God.

Psalms 76-78 are the suggested reading for today

Here is a taste

¹ My people, hear my teaching; listen to the words of my mouth.
² I will open my mouth with a parable; I will utter hidden things, things from of old—
³ things we have heard and known, things our ancestors have told us. ⁴ We will not
hide them from their descendants; we will tell the next generation the praiseworthy
deeds of the Lord, his power, and the wonders he has done.

Psalm 78:1-4 NIV

Abba…

I love Your stories and the lessons that they teach us. The more we hear them, the more we learn about You and about us. We are just like the people in the Bible; a bunch of sheep in search of a shepherd. Thank You for rescuing us, feeding us on Your Word, protecting us from wild animals that stalk us; leading us into green pastures and beside still waters; taking us up and around the hill to the top where we can see clearly Your plan for our lives. You are a wonderful story teller!

Amen

Day 28

Heaven's Realm Invading Earth's Realm

Prophetically, there is something on the other side of all these disturbances that are making up the 24-hour-news-cycle that we live in today.

We are living in the days where Heaven's Realm is invading Earth's Realm and there is war in the heavenlies. We have never lived through something such as this before. We have seen the guns-of-war, with uniforms and flags from different countries and men fighting one another; loss of lives; and the devastation caused by declarations of war. One nation against another; it is the way of man.

But we have never seen with our own eyes what we have been experiencing recently in America since the end of May of 2020. We are watching demonic spirits coming from the flesh of men and women. Many, are not even allies of the demons, but useful flesh for the demonic realm to operate from.

What does the Bible say about His Kingdom coming?

> *Now when He was asked by the Pharisees when the kingdom of God would*
> *come, He answered them and said, "The kingdom of God does not come*
> *with observation;*
> Luke 17:30

We need to see *mulberry trees being pulled out by their roots and cast into the sea...* all because we are exercising mustard-seed-sized-faith by the declaration and decree. When we do the things Yeshua said, we will experience His Kingdom coming and we will be aware of it!

Humans have the gift of speech. It can be a good thing; an eloquent thing; a funny thing; an educational thing; a musical thing; a spiritual thing; or a very destructive weapon. Our speech can build up something good. We can lend our energies in agreement with our words of approval or agreement.

James wrote about the weapon that we all wield... our tongue. It is how we express our words. It can be used for good or it can cause destruction all around us. We must be aware of the words coming from our mouths; they feed one side of the battle or the other. Your words can be used to praise God, ask for His help. If they are expressing fear and agreement with what the enemy is doing, then those words are feeding the enemy... much like cancer will feed on sugar. *Selah*

Like the signs posted in Rocky Mountain National Park that say, "don't feed the animals in the park", neither should we be 'feeding' the enemy. Words of fear, or doubt, or hatred come into agreement with what the powers and principalities are doing. Again, these are the things that feed the enemy!

The weapons of our warfare are not carnal, but are mighty for the pulling down of strongholds. These strongholds are deceptive deeds of the enemy. They are the things that should be torn down, pulled up by the roots and thrown into the sea that Yeshua spoke of.

Your picture belongs on a "Most Wanted Poster" in the Post Office: **Believers Wanted**... who will speak and pray in faith. Believers who will use their authority to tear down strongholds... teaming up with God's warring angels... in bringing revival to this generation.

Is this what *Jericho* was all about? No wonder, the Children of Israel were commanded not to say a word as they marched around the city of Jericho the week prior to Yom Teruah. For nearly a week, they marched around the city once each day and didn't say a word as the priest sounded trumpets with the Teruah sound. Then on the seventh day, after seven circulations around the city, they shouted, and the sound of their voice and the sound of the shofars caused the walls of evil to fall down. The power of the tongue, the power of words cannot be underestimated; it brings about good and evil. What comes out of our mouths is as powerful as what comes out of the shofar. Use both wisely…

Psalms 79-81 are the suggested reading today

Here is a taste

Come back, we beg of you, O God of the armies of heaven, and bless us.
Look down from heaven and see our plight and care for this your vine!
[15] Protect what you yourself have planted, this son you have raised for yourself.
[16] For we are chopped and burned by our enemies.
May they perish at your frown. [1]
[7] Strengthen the man you love, the son of your choice,
[18] and we will never forsake you again.
Revive us to trust in you.

Psalm 89:14-18 TLB

Abba… teach us about this weapon of our tongue. We need to use it appropriately. Forgive us for when we have aided and abetted the enemy. Forgive us when we have hurt someone with it. We are in need of going to speech class with You. Teach us what to say and when to speak.

Amen

Day 29

The Party You Don't Want to Miss

The words one speaks are a result of what is in that person's mind, will and heart. Does that pertain to God as well? Let's take a closer look. In the Gospel account of the Book of John, we are told that the Word of God was with God in the beginning. Yeshua's presence with man on earth was a result of what was in the mind, will and heart of God. This Divine Word became a human… in the body of Yeshua. He came to do the will of God.

Think about this… the very Presence that hovered over the Ark of the Covenant in the Tabernacle at Mt. Sinai became a human being, while maintaining His connection with the Holy Spirit. Therefore, the One True God of Israel, the Holy Spirit, was the Father and the Son.

In Chapter 1 of John there are 7 statements as to who Yeshua is: **Lamb of God** v.29; **Son of God** v.34; **Rabbi** v.38; **Messiah** v.41; **Jesus of Nazareth** v.45; **King** of Israel v.49; **Son of Man** v.51. This is yet another example of the number SEVEN in action.

Here in the first chapter of the Gospel of John: The fully human Yeshua, from Nazareth is the Messiah, King and Teacher (rabbi) of Israel, as well as the Son of God and the Lamb slain for our sins.

This Teacher, Messiah, and God in the flesh goes to a Wedding in Cana where He prophetically turns water, in ceremonial jugs, into the best wine. Our Rabbi is teaching us about the great party to come… described in Isaiah 25. It sounds just like a wedding party.

…the Lord Almighty will spread a wondrous feast for everyone around the world—a delicious feast of good food, with clear, well-aged wine and choice beef. [7] At that time he will remove the cloud of gloom, the pall of death that hangs over the earth; [8] he will swallow up death forever. The Lord God will wipe away all tears and take away forever all insults and mockery against his land and people. The Lord has spoken—he will surely do it! [9] In that day the people will proclaim, "This is our God in whom we trust, for whom we waited. Now at last he is here." What a day of rejoicing! Isaiah 25"6-9 TLB

This wedding at Cana is also a prophetic picture of His Bride. But the Bride, at this wedding in Cana, is the only member of the wedding party not mentioned! Who is the Bride? Yeshua told His mother that His time had not yet come, nor was there a Bride present. Well, now is the time, and the hour, for the Bride to be showing up. The Bride/Partner of Yeshua is… alive and learning… on planet earth today; a member of the last generation to see the fall moedim or appointed times fulfilled in the land of the living.

That party is one we don't want to miss. And it is good to be ready. And this is the season to get ready… for He is returning for the Bride; perhaps soon. *Matthew 25: [6] "At midnight someone announced, 'The bridegroom is coming! Come and meet him!'*

The Word of God is also alive and well on planet earth today; and it is sharper than any two-edged sword. Let's make sure our minds, wills and hearts have been prepared during these days of repentance.

Psalms 82-84 is the suggested reading for today

Here is a taste

[10] For a day in Your courts is better than a thousand.
I would rather be a doorkeeper in the house of my God
Than dwell in the tents of wickedness.
[11] For the Lord God is a sun and shield;
The Lord will give grace and glory;
No good thing will He withhold
From those who walk uprightly.[12] O Lord of hosts,
Blessed is the man who trusts in You!

Psalm 84: 10-12

Abba…

We want to be invited to this party! We want to go out to meet You as You arrive. Thank You for allowing us to be part of this generation. We are looking, waiting, wanting You to return to us. Oh… and may I have my steak medium with a little pink in the middle? Amen

Day 30

Grace ~ a Terrible Thing to Waste

Let's look at a word we have all used time and time again: **GRACE**. Oh, sure we know what it means... unmerited favor. Right...? Right? The concept of - *the grace of God demonstrated toward man*- is what I want to look at today. It is the concept of having favor 'in the eyes of YHVH'. It is through grace that He sees His children. We cannot do anything to earn it. Grace just is; in fact, there is an anointing for grace.

It is His grace that brings us:

- salvation
- forgiveness
- healing
- miracles
- wealth

God even says in *Deuteronomy 8* [18] *"And you shall remember the Lord your God, for it is He who gives you power to get wealth, that He may establish His covenant which He swore to your fathers, as it is this day.*

The wealth of a nation or an individual is all by His grace... to establish the Covenant that He made with the fathers: Abraham, Isaac, and Jacob. Can you see why the *'Joseph'* and *'Judah'* countries are among the wealthy nations? Their wealth is a byproduct of the anointing of His grace. We have no control of when it happens; we are the recipients of His grace. Anointing always accompanies His grace. Grace is on everything He does; that is why we can't earn it!

It is the time for the Harvest of the Nations, and it will be by His Grace and accompanied by His Anointing. He said, "The harvest is great but the laborers are few." It is God's grace that accepts our repentance and by His grace, revival will soon to follow.

Abba, we desire the Aaronic Blessing to be graciously upon each and every one of us for the sake of Your Kingdom:

24-26 'May the Lord bless and protect you; may the Lord's face radiate with joy because of you; may he be gracious to you, show you his favor, and give you his peace.' Numbers 6   TLB

This is not by our doing whatsoever but by the grace of the hand of Yeshua, who holds all things together by His power. If there is an Assignment of Revival for this last Generation then it will be by the Anointing of His Grace.

We can certainly call out to Him for it. In fact, that is what we should be doing! Once in every generation, there is an open door for revival. On the other side of the storms and fires and floods and riots is the other side of the rainbow, and His anointing for grace upon our land. It is part of the benefits of being the Children of God. We have no idea how powerful our authority as Believers is and how Big the Covenant is. Perhaps it is time to find out.

One man of you shall chase a thousand, for the Lord your God is He who fights for you, as He promised you. Joshua 23:10

And God said, "This is the sign of the covenant that I make between me and you and every living creature that is with you, for all future generations: I have set my bow in the cloud, and it shall be a sign of the covenant between me and the earth. Genesis 9:12-13

Psalms 85-87 are the suggested reading for today

Here is a taste

[10] Mercy and truth have met together;
Righteousness and peace have kissed.
[11] Truth shall spring out of the earth,
And righteousness shall look down from heaven.
[12] Yes, the LORD will give what is good;
And our land will yield its increase.
[13] Righteousness will go before Him,
And shall make His footsteps our pathway.

Psalm 85: 10-12

Abba,

Let us play a part in this harvest. Let us have clean hands, and a pure heart and willingness to work in Your field. You will supply all of our needs according to Your riches in glory. We come to Your throne and bow before You. Amen

Day 31

Bonus Day

Bonus Day... In case the moon is hiding... some years it does! God is in control of time.

Yom Teruah, The Day of Sounding is the day that no man knows; for the moon can reappear on the day 29 or 30 or 31.

Yeshua, King of Israel. Yeshua, Priest of the Most High. He is our God. He shall return with a trumpet sound and we shall behold Him in all of His glory. Sounds pretty good! (no pun intended)

But now we know that it is the *SOUND* that comes from the trumpet or shofar that is important. When Yeshua returns, if the sound of the Last Trump is the Tekia Gadola, that will be a loud and long blast.

Yom Teruah (Feast of Trumpets) is to be associated with the Coronation of a King, specifically our King Yeshua. Not only is He our King (from royalty, and can return anytime) - but those of His Father's House will rule and reign with Him.

We American Protestant Believers don't know what it is like to live under a king or be answerable to a priest. We were not brought up that way. Maybe that's good, but nonetheless, we can't relate to either king or priest. All we can do is read about it from historical accounts or use our imagination or watch a movie about it. But, look at what Yeshua has for those who repent and open the door to Him to be King and Priest in their lives:

As many as I love, I rebuke and chasten. Therefore be zealous and repent. 20 Behold, I stand at the door and knock. If anyone hears My voice and opens the door, I will come in to him and dine with him, and he with Me. 21 To him who overcomes I will grant to sit with Me on My throne, as I also overcame and sat down with My Father on His throne. Revelation 3:19

There is real physical land, involved in the redemption, which pours forth from the pages of the Bible. His Kingdom will be made **manifest** on the earth [Hmmm....] Is that what we are watching take place now? If so, are we participating in it: With our deeds? With our words? With our faith? Are we declaring and decreeing and proclaiming that the King is coming? Do we believe it? Do we understand it? Ahhhhh… so many questions, so little time!

Yeshua, born King of Israel, came the first time to perform the duties of the Priest: overseeing the sacrifice of the Lamb of God. He stayed alive on the cross, at **Passover**, long enough to absorb the sins of all men until He declared, *"It is finished!"*. The sinless Man became leavened on our behalf, He bore our sins; He was pierced for our iniquities. No wonder we eat **Unleavened Bread** for a week! He lay in a grave for three nights and three days and became the **First Fruit** offering with His Resurrection.

Having accomplished that task, He cleared the way for the Spirit of God to return and, occupy man. Once again, the Spirit of the Living God would fill and indwell those who would believe and accept what God's Son had come to do. Yeshua was the One that was sent from heaven to die for our sins, and remove the law of sin and death. The Holy Spirit was sent to fill us and empower us to be Overcomers. This new indwelling arrangement was fulfilled fifty days after the Resurrection at **Shavuot**. Thus, He fulfilled all of the Spring Moedim. Yeshua gave us something to believe in! Yeshua is form/ Holy Spirit is function.

So you also, when you see these things happening, know that the kingdom of God is near. Assuredly, I say to you, this generation will by no means pass away till all things take place. Luke 21:31-32

Psalms 88-90 are the suggested reading for today

Here is a taste

Return, O Lord! How long? And have compassion on Your servants.
14 Oh, satisfy us early with Your mercy,
That we may rejoice and be glad all our days!
15 Make us glad according to the days in which You have afflicted us,
The years in which we have seen evil.
16 Let Your work appear to Your servants,
And Your glory to their children.
17 And let the beauty of the Lord our God be upon us,
And establish the work of our hands for us;
Yes, establish the work of our hands.

Psalm 90: 13-17

Abba… This generation has seen many things; perhaps like other generations have. But now the earth is groaning for the sons of God to be revealed. We long to see Your Spirit poured out on Your sons and daughters. We long to see people turning and returning to You. We long to see healing take place in the midst of so much decay, infection, and spiritual leprosy that is right in our midst. Complete the Feast Cycle and return to Your people even as Your people return to You. Amen

YOM TERUAH

Day of Trumpets

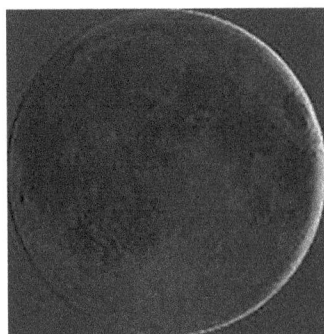

The Waxing Crescent and the Mystery of the New Moon.

At the close of the month of Elul and the eve of the month of Tishri, the Moon will be in a **Waxing Crescent** Phase. A Waxing Crescent is the first Phase after the New Moon and is a great time to see the features of the moon's surface. During this phase, the Moon can be seen in the western sky after the sun dips below the horizon at sunset. The moon is close to the sun in the sky and mostly dark except for the right edge of the moon which becomes brighter as the days get closer to the next phase which is a First Quarter with a 50% illumination.

Erev Yom Teruah approaches. To Sound the Shofar at the Coronation of a King is customary. To be aware of this function of this appointed time is important. The month of Elul comes to an end today and beginning tomorrow, we enter the Ten Days of Awe.

Here is yet another look at the blast sounds coming from the Shofar as seen through Jewish eyes: The combined Shevarim – Teruah Sounds… (3 short and 9 staccato) represent the out-cry and sobs and groanings that are beyond screaming. These are compared to a forlorn child in a distant country who has forgotten the language of his people and his father - the King. Upon his return and face-to-face encounter with his father, his only means of communication is this sobbing cry. The father recognizes his son and draws him close. (That sounds like the prodigal son returning to his father… and such are we)

Even so, if we have lost our way to speak with our Father, the shofar will speak for us. As we draw near the time for Yom Teruah, remember it is about our hearts yielding to and turning to God… our Father… and us saying to Him, "We will hear and we will do."

Tonight, we will look for the New Moon and blow the sounds of the shofar. As we look at the night sky and see the wonderful sign in the heavens as depicted in Revelation 12, remember that we are created in His image. Let's remember that Yeshua was the Son given to us, for us, so that He could be with us.

We have been created in God's image. As we draw close to Him during this season, let's also remember what He has done for us in sending Yeshua to pay the price for our redemption. We have been born again in His likeness to do the things He did. May the sounds of the Shofar this evening as we watch, look for, and see the New Moon also remind us of the words of Isaiah 9:

A child will be born for us. A son will be given to us.
The government will rest on his shoulders.
He will be named:
Wonderful Counselor,
Mighty God,
Everlasting Father,
Prince of Peace.
⁷ His government and peace will have unlimited growth.
He will establish David's throne and kingdom.
He will uphold it with justice and righteousness now and forever.
The Lord of Armies is determined to do this!

Psalms 94-96 are the suggested reading for today

Here is a taste

Sing a new song to the Lord!
Let the whole world sing to the Lord!
² Sing to the Lord and praise his name!
Tell the good news every day about how he saves us!
³ Tell all the nations how wonderful he is!
Tell people everywhere about the amazing things he does.
⁴ The Lord is great and worthy of praise.
He is more awesome than any of the "gods."

⁵ All the "gods" in other nations are nothing but statues,
but the Lord made the heavens.
⁶ He lives in the presence of glory and honor.
His Temple is a place of power and beauty.
⁷ Praise the Lord, all people of every nation;
praise the Lord's glory and power.
⁸ Give the Lord praise worthy of his glory!
Come, bring your offerings into his courtyard.
⁹ Worship the Lord in all his holy beauty.
Everyone on earth should tremble before him.
¹⁰ Tell the nations that the Lord is King!
The world stands firm and cannot be moved.
He will judge all people fairly.
¹¹ Let the heavens rejoice and the earth be happy!
Let the sea and everything in it shout for joy!
¹² Let the fields and everything in them be happy!
Let the trees in the forest sing for joy
¹³ when they see the Lord coming!
He is coming to rule the world.
He will rule all the nations of the world
with justice and fairness.

Psalm 96:1-13

Abba...

Thank You for going to all the trouble to create us, sustain us, redeem us, provide for us and love us. No longer a babe in a manger are You. No longer an itinerate Rabbi are You. No longer a man on trial are You.

You are the risen Son of God. You are the Prophet who was to come. You are the Priest of the Most High God in the order of Malki-tsedek. You are King of Kings and LORD of Lords. You are God.

And me... I am blessed to belong to You. Even so, Come Lord Jesus.

Amen

DAYS OF AWE

The Days of Awe are the first 10 days of the seventh month of Tishri; and they are a continuation of the days of repentance before God. The 30-day month of Elul *and* the ten days of Tishri make the 40 Days of Repentance, ending with the Day of Atonement (or Yom Kippur.)

It is said that the Book of Judgement is opened on the Day of Trumpets (Yom Teruah). On the Jewish clock, one has until the Day of Yom Kippur to make sure his name is written in God's Book of Life.

Christians have a much different view of this book. Our names are written in the Lamb's Book of Life, Halleluyah!

So, friends, the "Elul Zone" is ending and we step into the Ten Days of Awe. We now look for the first sliver of New Moon announcing the beginning of the new month, Tishri. The fall Feasts of: Trumpets, Yom Kippur and Tabernacles all fall within the days of this seventh month called, Tishri. It is the time for the ingathering of the harvest.

The last day of Elul… is also… the eve of Tishri one. We wait, and we watch for the New Moon in the western sky with great anticipation. There it is! The moon is just above the horizon soon after the sun sets. It is always with great joy and anticipation to watch for the moon to appear and then announce it to everyone with the sounds of the shofar. The new month has begun. Yom Teruah – Day of Trumpets, is the only Biblical feast day that falls on the first day of the month. (Yep, in the Bible a day begins in the evening!)

Another name for this day is – *the day that no man knows*. The moon must be sited before the new month can be announced. That ole moon can hide one, two or three days! Seeing the moon is important because only then can they plan for Yom Kippur (Day of Atonement) which will fall on the tenth day of this new month. These are days to be aware of and to make sure you are in right standing with God before the Judge *takes His seat on Yom Kippur.*

We all know that Judgement is coming and is knocking at the door. These Days of Awe are appropriately named. Oh, I'll be you thought Judgement is about you. If you are one of God's kids, then this Judgement is *for* you. The enemy of our souls that is causing so much trouble is being exposed, uncovered and is about to be judged from the Court in Heaven.

We want to be ready with clean hands and pure hearts standing in the Presence of the LORD, when He renders judgement in our favor. That is why these days of repentance are so important. The accuser of the brethren is about to be found guilty in God's Courtroom. Yes, these are exiting days we are living in!

> [3] *Who may ascend into the hill of the Lord? Or who may stand in His holy place?* [4] *He who has clean hands and a pure heart, Who has not lifted up his soul to an idol, Nor sworn deceitfully.* [5] *He shall receive blessing from the Lord, And righteousness from the God of his salvation. Psalm 24:3-4*

> [14] *"Because he has set his love upon Me, therefore I will deliver him; I will set him on high, because he has known My name.* [15] *He shall call upon Me, and I will answer him; I will be with him in trouble; I will deliver him and honor him.* [16] *With long life I will satisfy him, And show him My salvation." Psalm 91: 14-16*

Day 1 of the Days of Awe

Sound the Trumpet

On Yom Teruah (Feast of Trumpets), a traditional prayer called the Avinu, (Our Father) is recited. On this day we acknowledge the gift of forgiveness. But YHVH is much more than *Forgiver*. He is *Redeemer*. He is *Deliverer*. He is strong in might and strong in battle. This shofar blast is not simply to call us to repentance. It is to remind us of why we are called to repentance. It is a reminder of what comes after… Victory over the enemy!

Imagine, if you will, being in a Conestoga wagon in the nineteenth century, heading across the great American Plains... seeking your fortune and future. Over the next rise, in the not-too-distant sunlit landscape, you see a gang of outlaws that is directly in your path. Your eyes get big, your heart is beating wildly, you have nowhere to hide, and you can't run fast enough to escape. Sounds like a nightmare, right?

All of a sudden you hear the sound of a trumpet sounding off in the distance. Here they come, riding fast and raising a dust storm as they come. You expect to see some kind of army, but all you see is dust swirling about. The sound of a trumpet is blaring. You hear the sound of crisp, clear, quick staccato tones. Your fear is swallowed up in hope; and certain death is swallowed up in victory. This is the essence of what the sound of the shofar should do for those who hear it.

Each year we gather, we have been surrounded by the enemy of our soul. But then, the shofar sounds and we realize the King is coming with His army to bring total victory against our enemy.

When the shofar blasts on Yom Teruah, our hearts are reminded that with every year that passes, the King is getting closer and closer. One day soon we will hear the Great Shofar Sound and the enemy will be vanquished. Yom Teruah is intended to keep us watching for His deliverance as we are set free. I am loving these Rehearsals!

Psalm 97 is the suggested reading for today

Here is a taste

You who love the Lord, hate evil!
He preserves the souls of His saints;
He delivers them out of the hand of the wicked.
Psalm 97:10

Abba…

Thank You for giving us Your Feast Days to remember You throughout the Year. They are so full of meaning and information and teaching about Messiah. I love having learned from You that Yeshua didn't just show up one day to be Messiah. It was all planned out by You: When He would come, Where He would come, Why He would come, How He would come and Who He is… the Great I AM in the flesh.

Forgive us for ignoring the lessons from Your feasts for so long. We didn't know. Our Messiah even died for all of the "but I didn't knows". Yes, we have been ignorant of Your ways, yet ignorance is curable. Thank You for teaching us… slowly but surely Who you really are.

Amen

96

Day 2 of the Days of Awe

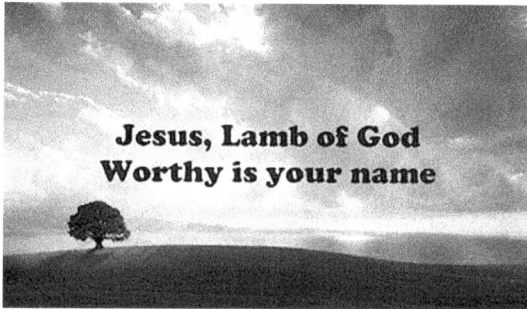

Jesus, Lamb of God
Worthy is your name

Lamb's Book of Life

Now, we move on toward the next Moed, Yom Kippur... which will be on the tenth day of Tishri. This appointed time addresses the courtroom scene of and is associated with *judgment*. In Jewish understanding and teaching, Yom Kippur is when the 'Books of Judgement' are closed. Your fate for the following year depends on your name being written in the Book of Life.

Well, my friends, Yeshua says your name is inscribed on His hands. (Isaiah 49:16). Your name has been written in the Lamb's Book of Life. What Lamb?

You know:

- the Lamb that was slain from the foundation of the world
- the Lamb that Abraham told Isaac, "God will provide Himself the lamb for the burnt offering"
- the Lamb that John the Baptist told those coming to get baptized, "See, the Lamb of God that takes away the sin of the world."
- the Lamb who is LORD of Lords and King of kings
- the Lamb who is the also the scapegoat provided by God
- the Lamb who stayed alive on the cross long enough to absorb all the sin of the world

Rejoice and Bless His Name forevermore! Your name has been written in the **Lamb's Book of Life.** He also has a Book of Remembrance that He writes the wonderful things you do for His Kingdom. He will go over it with you one day. Hmmm....

"Then those who feared the LORD spoke to one another, and the LORD gave attention and heard it, and a book of remembrance was written before Him for those who fear the LORD and who esteem His name. 'They will be Mine,' says the LORD of hosts, 'on the day that I prepare My own possession, and I will spare them as a man spares his own son who serves him. So you will again distinguish between the righteous and the wicked, between one who serves God and one who does not serve Him.'" Malachi 3:16

Psalms 98-99 are the suggested reading for today

Here is a taste

4This mighty King is determined to give justice.
Fairness is the touchstone of everything he does.
He gives justice throughout Israel.
5 Exalt the Lord our holy God! Bow low before his feet.

Psalm 99:4-5

Abba...

Thank You that my name is written in the Lamb's Book of Life. You are Life and Love. Help me to have more pages in my book. I want to live my life for You.

Amen

Day 3 of the Days of Awe

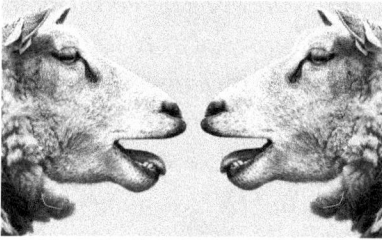

Two Goats-
One for God / One for you

On Yom Kippur, YHVH commanded the Priest to bring two animals for sacrifice at the Tabernacle as described in Leviticus 16. After sacrificing a bull on his own behalf, he would take two goats on behalf of the nation. After casting lots, deciding which goat would be sacrificed to the LORD, he sacrificed this chosen animal as the sin offering. The second was called the *Azazel* or scapegoat. The priest would symbolically lay the sins of the people on the head of this goat and this scapegoat would then be led away by a 'fit man' to a place outside of the camp.

This particular sacrifice would occur once a year, and was just a temporary covering for sin for the nation. Year after year the Israelites repeated this tradition to ensure sins were covered and names were sealed in the Book of Life. But there has been no Temple for over 2000 years and no sacrifice for Atonement either.

Yom Kippur, or the Day of Atonement, was always meant to be a symbol of pointing to something to come—something much greater and something to celebrate. That something is a 'Someone' - Yeshua! He came and willingly laid down His life for the sins of all people. In doing so, His blood was splashed all over the streets of Jerusalem, the City of the Great King. The blood of Yeshua, which we claim for ourselves, atoned for our sin; His resurrection provided for our salvation.

- **Without** the shedding of blood there is no remission of sin.
- **With** the shedding of His blood there is no further sacrifice for sin.

The scapegoat was to be taken, by a 'fit' man, outside the camp and led away… carrying all the sins of the nation symbolically on his head. Much of Israel has missed its visitation by the 'Someone'. We pray for the revelation of the Jewish Messiah to come to them.

In Leviticus 16, different words are used to describe the sin of God's covenant people: *uncleanliness, transgressions, iniquities, and sins*. All four words are plural to show the vastness, frequency and utter depravity of humanity. Yeshua dealt with all of them at the cross.

> *Isaiah 53: [10]Yet it pleased the Lord to bruise Him; He has put Him to grief. When You make His soul an offering for sin, He shall see Hi seed, He shall prolong His days, And the pleasure of the Lord shall prosper in His hand. [11] He shall see the labor of His soul and be satisfied. By His Knowledge My Righteous Servant shall justify many, For He shall bear their iniquities. [12] Therefore I will divide Him a portion with the great, And He shall divide the spoil with the strong, Because He poured out His soul unto death, And He was numbered with the transgressors, And He bore the sin of many, And made intercession for the transgressors.*

Yeshua is the *fit man* and was taken outside the camp and to carry our sins away. We are blessed to plead the blood of the sacrifice Lamb, Yeshua, over our lives. We are forgiven and we are loved by the One who created us. He certainly went to a lot of trouble and time and pain to pay the price for His Bride. His strategies are working and His tactics will result in the salvation of many.

Psalms 100-102 are the suggested reading for today

Here is a taste

Shout with joy before the Lord, O earth! [2] Obey him gladly; come before him, singing with joy. [3] Try to realize what this means—the Lord is God! He made us— we are his people, the sheep of his pasture. [4] Go through his open gates with great thanksgiving; enter his courts with praise. Give thanks to him and bless his name. [5] For the Lord is always good. He is always loving and kind, and his faithfulness goes on and on to each succeeding generation.

Psalm 100: 1-5

Abba,

Thank You for the blood of the Passover Lamb, Yeshua, who also was the Fit Man to carry my sins away outside the camp. Passover and Yom Kippur are linked forever because of Yeshua, the Messiah. You delivered us from the curse of sin and separation from You. Halleluyah!

Amen

Day 4 of the Days of Awe

Forgiveness

Using Words to Communicate

Romans 12: 17 Never pay back evil for evil. Do things in such a way that everyone can see you are honest clear through. 18 Don't quarrel with anyone. Be at peace with everyone, just as much as possible.

James 1:19 Dear brothers, don't ever forget that it is best to listen much, speak little, and not become angry; 20 for anger doesn't make us good, as God demands that we must be.

Romans 5:1 So now, since we have been made right in God's sight by faith in his promises, we can have real peace with him because of what Jesus Christ our Lord has done for us. 2 For because of our faith, he has brought us into this place of highest privilege where we now stand, and we confidently and joyfully look forward to actually becoming all that God has had in mind for us to be.

Paul and James remind us to be quick to listen, slow to speak, and slow in becoming angry. That is good advice. Being angry is not becoming to anyone. If it is possible to live at peace, as far as it depends on you - then do it.

At times in your life there will be those who are determined to oppose you - without good cause. At times, you have made a contribution to the dust-up. Words are what we use to communicate with and at times they can get away from us. Do what you can to restore relationships. If you try and it doesn't happen, then God will not hold you responsible.

Forgive, move on, and don't despair. We live in a fallen world and there will always be loose ends. We will always be rearranging the cards that we have been dealt. Play them wisely. Beloved, we will be tested. We would do well to remember that. If we are wise, we will let the Holy Spirit, who dwells in us, pass the test for us. Selah

Psalms 103-105 are the suggested reading for today

Here is a taste

²Bless the LORD, O my soul, and forget not all his benefits,
³who forgives all your iniquity, who heals all your diseases,
⁴who redeems your life from the pit, who crowns you with steadfast love and mercy,
⁵who satisfies you with good so that your youth is renewed like the eagle's.
⁶The LORD works righteousness and justice for all who are oppressed.
⁷He made known his ways to Moses, his acts to the people of Israel.
⁸The LORD is merciful and gracious, slow to anger and abounding in steadfast love.
⁹He will not always chide, nor will he keep his anger forever.
¹⁰He does not deal with us according to our sins, nor repay us according to our iniquities.
¹¹For as high as the heavens are above the earth, so great is his steadfast love toward those who fear him;
¹²as far as the east is from the west, so far does he remove our transgressions from us.

Psalm 103   ESV

Abba…

We are a virtual dictionary of words. We use them all day long, from shortly after we get up until we lay our head on the pillow. Some of us even talk in our sleep! Help us to throw out the words that are not helpful, or that treat others lightly. The idea of being at peace with everyone sounds like a wonderful idea… and yet it also seems difficult to achieve. Help us to change our mind about being at peace with others as far as we are able. People are Your specialty. Help us to see them that way and to treat them that way also.

Amen

Day 5 of the Days of Awe

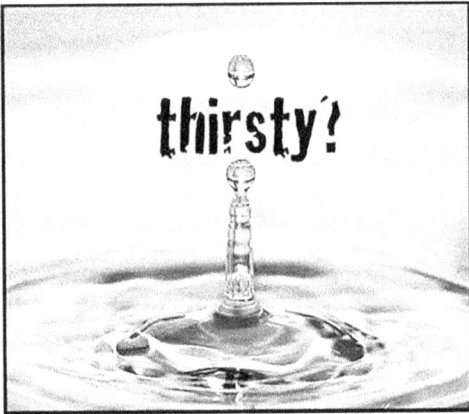

thirsty?

Times of Refreshing~
On the Way

Water is by far the most common thing on earth. It fills the rivers and the seas. We don't **live in** the water but we need to **take in** water to live. We use water every day and could not live without it; we drink it, bathe in it, cook with it, sail on it - well, you get the idea.

But have you stopped to think that the water in your glass, today, has been around since creation… to sustain your life? God is not making any new water. After all, He created for 6 days and on the 7th day, He rested. The water that is here has always been here. Talk about recycling!

Let's take that a step further. Everything you see around you has come out of the earth. Everything that man has made… from *awnings* to *zippers*… has been made from materials that come from the earth. Even mankind has come from the materials that make up the earth!

Let's take that a step further. Mankind, who comes from the earth, has a sin problem. This comes from our fallen nature. We are all in the same boat. ***For all have sinned and fallen short of the glory of God***. That brings us to the remedy. We need a remedy because the fallen sin nature is what separates us from God.

Yeshua stands at the door and knocks. He stands there with a gift for mankind. It is the only gift that was not made from the materials of the earth. This is the precious gift of His blood for the cleansing of our sin. His blood did not come from His mother… but from His Father (ultimately). On the cross, when the Roman soldier pierced His side with a spear, it was blood and water that came out. The blood from heaven and water from His earthly humanity give us two witnesses.

Revelation 1:5 says, "To Him who loved us, and washed us from our sins in His own blood."

John 19:34, "But one of the soldiers pierced His side with a spear, and immediately blood and water came out."

Yeshua's uncorrupted Blood, in His veins; and the Spirit of God, in Him accomplished the following:

- His blood paid the price… to take away and remove the taint of our sin
- He conquered/overcame the curse of death.
- He was then, and only then, able to return the Ruach (Holy Spirit) to mankind.

Be full of expectation, friends. Something wonderful is on the way. Times of refreshing are on the way; as refreshing as a cool drink of water given in the Name of Yeshua. Let's receive it and say, "Thank You".

The generation that is seeing these things come to pass shall not pass away until everything comes to pass. He's at the door with a gift for you. Answer the door! He has the gift of life, and love, and healing, and grace. It's a package deal.

Psalms 106-108 are the suggested reading for today

Here is a taste

²⁸ Then they cried to the Lord in their trouble,
and he delivered them from their distress.
²⁹ He made the storm be still,
and the waves of the sea were hushed.
³⁰ Then they were glad that the waters[c] were quiet,
and he brought them to their desired haven.
³¹ Let them thank the Lord for his steadfast love,
for his wondrous works to the children of man!
³² Let them extol him in the congregation of the people,
and praise him in the assembly of the elders.

Psalm 107:28 ESV

Abba...

Thank You for the most precious gift of all... Life. We have physical life because a man and a woman came together and created a baby. We have spiritual life because You came in a body prepared to be the sin offering and blood substitute for our sin. The blood that came from heaven and cleansed us from sin made it possible for the Holy Spirit to dwell with us and in us. What a Divine Gift indeed! You give it, we receive it. It is that perfectly simple. What can we say but... Thank You!

Amen

Day 6 of the Days of Awe

Don't Miss Out on the Prize

Perhaps you have heard the old story that goes something like this: A wealthy man had only one surviving son. The father was a good man and devoted to God. He was a man who knew the Word of God and tried to encourage his son to study also. However, the son was not interested in Biblical things and went his own way.

The father eventually passed away, leaving only his worn Bible to his son, as instructed by the man's lawyer. The son was both surprised and angry. He took the Bible, put it in a box, and placed it on the shelf of his closet.

Many years later, he was cleaning out that closet and found the Bible that had been there so very long. Feeling a little sentimental, he sat down and opened up the well-worn, Book. As he opened it, an envelope dropped out. Inside were instructions and a letter of love from his father as to how to obtain his inheritance. The son had missed out because he had not bothered to even open the Book, the most prized possession that his father owned. He had spent years being angry and feeling unloved for no other reason than he would not open the Bible.

How many people are in the same kind of predicament? If the Bible is not opened and not consulted and not studied, then how do we find out the wonderful news of being part of the children of Abraham?

So many words and concepts that we think come from the New Testament are Torah words that are for Abraham's kids: Like *Justice* and *Righteousness, Mercy* and *Grace, Faith* and *Trust, Hear* and *Obey*. It is in the pages of the Torah that these words are given meaning and application.

One thing we can be thankful for during these days of awe... leading up to Yom Kippur is that we are awaiting a favorable decision from the Righteous Judge. He is going to render judgment in your favor; your fine has been paid in full. You are about to get back what the guilty party has taken from you.

Psalms 109-111 are the suggested reading for today

Here is a taste

Praise the Lord!
I will give thanks to the Lord with my whole heart,
in the company of the upright, in the congregation.
² Great are the works of the Lord,
studied by all who delight in them.
³ Full of splendor and majesty is his work,
and his righteousness endures forever.
⁴ He has caused his wondrous works to be remembered;
the Lord is gracious and merciful.
⁵ He provides food for those who fear him;
he remembers his covenant forever.
⁶ He has shown his people the power of his works,
in giving them the inheritance of the nations.
⁷ The works of his hands are faithful and just;
all his precepts are trustworthy;
⁸ they are established forever and ever,
to be performed with faithfulness and uprightness.
⁹ He sent redemption to his people;
he has commanded his covenant forever.
Holy and awesome is his name!
¹⁰ The fear of the Lord is the beginning of wisdom;
all those who practice it have a good understanding.
His praise endures forever!

Psalm 111

Abba…

How many days, even years, have we wasted in getting to know who You really are? We are like the man who put the book away with the treasure buried inside. You have so much to teach us from the ancient words; many of them written 3500 years ago, or 3000 years ago, or 2500 years ago or 2000 years ago.

Turning our face toward You also means that we turn our eyes upon Your Word. We don't want to only wait for You to come and pick us up. We want to go out to meet You. We want to know what You are currently doing in our World. Cause Your face to shine upon us and give us Your light to see by. Forgive us for not wanting to come and sit at Your table, hear Your voice and learn the lessons that Your Word has for us. It's not too late. It's never too late with You!

Amen

Day 7 of the Days of Awe

Yom Kippur — One Day to Focus on God

Yom Kippur is just a few days away. Yom Kippur, a day of fasting. Why? It doesn't say to fast on this appointed time… this Moed… which is one of the High Holy days of Scripture. What it says is: 'you shall afflict your soul.' *27 "Also the tenth day of this seventh month shall be the Day of Atonement. It shall be a holy convocation for you; you shall afflict your soul…."*

What does that mean? One way to interpret that passage is that we must *"deny ourselves"* as we seek to focus on God. Fasting is the most readily available means of denying ourselves. Other ways of Fasting: from work, from TV, from the internet, from the telephone, from playing with Legos. There are many ways to 'afflict your soul' on the day of Yom Kippur. Once again, take the focus off of you and put it on God who, by grace and mercy and love saved you. This is what this day should be about.

Plan to spend this holy, separate, different-from-any-other-day, focusing on the One who saved you. It is Your day at His table; Your day in His Court Room. It's a day to celebrate your relationship with Yeshua. It is not punishment!!

This day… is one that the LORD has made; we should rejoice and be glad in it. This one day is when the chief Priest took off his colorful clothing, made of wool, and dressed only in white linen. He bathed... after each offering... and each time then dressed in clean linen. Linen, elsewhere, represents the righteous acts of the saints.

The priest took blood from a bull, for himself and his family, and then blood from a ram for the entire nation and brought the blood into the Holy of Holies to sprinkle upon the Mercy Seat of the Ark of the Covenant. This is the only time the Priest could enter that space - **once a year** - on Yom Kippur. The blood of bulls and goats is no longer necessary!

No longer is there a *curtain* between the altar-of-incense (your prayers) and the mercy seat. The veil has been rent and the way of mercy is obtainable and available to one and all. While it is good to deny our 'fleshly-selves' on this Day of Atonement, we also can celebrate and honor the day that the blood of Yeshua has atoned for our sin and we have obtained His Mercy and Grace in our lives. In fact, we can celebrate that we have been washed in the Blood of the Lamb and daily we can plead the blood of Yeshua over our lives.

So, give some thought about how you will spend this special day with the LORD. It is your time to spend. How will you invest it?

Psalms 112-114 are the suggested reading for today

Here is a taste

Praise the LORD!
Blessed is the man who fears the LORD,
who greatly delights in his commandments!
² His offspring will be mighty in the land;
the generation of the upright will be blessed.
³ Wealth and riches are in his house,
and his righteousness endures forever.
⁴ Light dawns in the darkness for the upright;
he is gracious, merciful, and righteous.
⁵ It is well with the man who deals generously and lends;
who conducts his affairs with justice.
⁶ For the righteous will never be moved;
he will be remembered forever.
⁷ He is not afraid of bad news;
his heart is firm, trusting in the LORD.
⁸ His heart is steady; he will not be afraid,
until he looks in triumph on his adversaries.
⁹ He has distributed freely; he has given to the poor;
his righteousness endures forever;
his horn is exalted in honor.

¹⁰ The wicked man sees it and is angry;
he gnashes his teeth and melts away;
the desire of the wicked will perish!

Psalm 112

Abba…

Yom Kippur is coming soon. It is a Court Date with You. I can't wait to see what You show me as I sit in Your chambers. Alone in Your court… me and You. Two more days. Can I even wait?

Amen

Day 8 of the Days of Awe

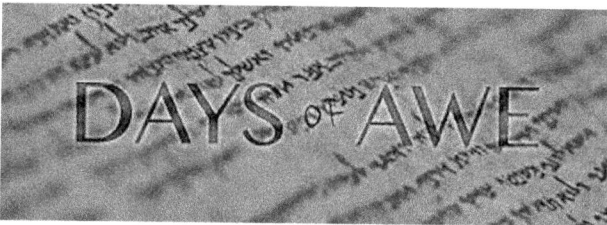

Celebrate Freedom

As Yom Kippur begins in two days, let's look at some questions that Isaiah put forth.

Is such the fast that I choose, a day for a person to humble himself? Is it to bow down his head like a reed, and to spread sackcloth and ashes under him? Will you call this a fast, and a day acceptable to the LORD? Is not this the fast that I choose: to loose the bonds of wickedness, to undo the straps of the yoke, to let the oppressed go free, and to break every yoke? Isaiah 57:5-6

Those of us who have been doing the Moedim for any period of time certainly associate Yom Kippur with fasting from food for the day. But, God's instruction about fasting here is not really about fasting from food at all. Instead, it is that ritual doesn't do anything unless it is accompanied by godly living.

Let's compare that passage to what Yeshua said on Yom Kippur…a year of Jubilee… when His ministry began.

[18] The Spirit of the Lord is upon me because he has anointed me to preach the gospel to the poor; he has sent me to heal the brokenhearted, to proclaim liberty to the captives and recovery of sight to the blind, to set at liberty those that are broken, [19] to proclaim the acceptable year of the Lord. Luke 4:18-19

Sounds like Yeshua is in total agreement with Isaiah. Actually, it is the other way around.

Yom Kippur looks like a day of FREEDOM and CELEBRATION! Even the Jewish art seems to indicate this! Let us remember that from the Passover in Egypt to the Passover of Yeshua, God's intention was to set the captives free whether from oppressive governments or sin that holds people in bondage.

The message of the Bible is Freedom. He starts with a man, gives him a family, promises him a land for his posterity; and then follows it up with this blessing: *"By Myself I have sworn, says the Lord, because you have done this thing, and have not withheld your son, your only son— [17] blessing I will bless you, and multiplying I will multiply your descendants as the stars of the heaven and as the sand which is on the seashore; and your descendants shall possess the gate of their enemies. [18] In your seed all the nations of the earth shall be blessed, because you have obeyed My voice."* *Genesis 22:16-18*

Psalms 115-117 are the suggested reading for today

Here is a taste

Truly I am your servant. Lord; I serve you just as my mother did; you have freed me from my chains. I will sacrifice a thank offering to you and call on the name of the Lord. I will fulfill my vows to the Lord in the presence of all his people in the courts of the house of the Lord – in your midst, Jerusalem. Praise the Lord

Psalm 116: 16-19

Abba,

I look forward to an official day with You. I know I can spend time with You every day. But this day, Yom Kippur, is set apart and different from all other days of the year. Praise Music, Bible Study, Pen and Notebook are being gathered. I am getting ready to spend the day with You and write down what You show me about Your family. Thank You for teaching me these things about Repentance over the last 40 days. You are my God and my Teacher and my Savior.

Amen

Day 9 of the Days of Awe

He Will Move Heaven and Earth to Keep His Promise to You

YOM KIPPUR is upon us... It will not be a surprise. We are prepared.

In Hebrew thought... One represents the Whole, which is especially seen on Yom Kippur. One ram was the sacrifice for the whole nation. One ram had the sins of the whole nation confessed over its head and sent off into the wilderness never to return. This is the flip side of the coin of the Passover Lamb (Yeshua). His blood shed for each of us... individually.

When you see these two feasts through the eyes of Messiah's work, it looks like this. He completed the assignments of these sacrifices and took our sin away:

- Messiah was the Goat for the LORD...
- Messiah was the Goat for the Nation...
- Messiah was the Lamb of God for every Individual...
- Messiah was the fit man who took the sin of the world outside the camp...

The blood of His sacrifice was shed for my sin, your sin, our sin. Without the shedding of blood there is no remission of sin. Yep, He loved His creation so much that He was willing to buy it back with His own blood.

There is a great example in Psalm 18. If King David represents the whole of Israel, then his prayer to God counts for you too! After so much warfare and many difficult days, David cries out to God. God's response is to move heaven and earth to get to David and save him. **Read** and **see** and **hear** and **feel** and **understand**: God is not mad at His children… those who are truly His. He will come and rescue and help and save them from their enemies. Yep, He is that God!

The lesson here is that we don't want to be at enmity with God nor with one another. You are His Beloved! So, step into David's sandals and read Psalm 18 as though his answer from God is for you too… because it is! Here are some excerpts to get you started.

Psalm 18 - I will love You, O Lord, my strength.² The Lord is my rock and my fortress and my deliverer; My God, my strength, in whom I will trust; My shield and the horn of my salvation, my stronghold. ³ I will call upon the Lord, who is worthy to be praised; So shall I be saved from my enemies.

………….

³⁵ You have also given me the shield of Your salvation; Your right hand has held me up, Your gentleness has made me great. ³⁶ You enlarged my path under me, So my feet did not slip. ³⁷ I have pursued my enemies and overtaken them; Neither did I turn back again till they were destroyed. ³⁸ I have wounded them, So that they could not rise; They have fallen under my feet.

………….

³⁹ For You have armed me with strength for the battle; You have subdued under me those who rose up against me. ⁴⁰ You have also given me the necks of my enemies, So that I destroyed those who hated me. ⁴¹ They cried out, but there was none to save; Even to the Lord, but He did not answer them.

………….

⁴⁹ Therefore I will give thanks to You, O Lord, among the Gentiles, And sing praises to Your name. ⁵⁰ Great deliverance He gives to His king, And shows mercy to His anointed, to David and his descendants forevermore.

Selah

Psalm 118 is the reading for today

Here is the whole meal

Oh give thanks to the Lord, for he is good; for his steadfast love endures forever!

² Let Israel say, "His steadfast love endures forever."
³ Let the house of Aaron say, "His steadfast love endures forever."
⁴ Let those who fear the Lord say, "His steadfast love endures forever."

⁵ Out of my distress I called on the Lord; the Lord answered me and set me free.
⁶ The Lord is on my side; I will not fear. What can man do to me?
⁷ The Lord is on my side as my helper; I shall look in triumph on those who hate me.

⁸ It is better to take refuge in the Lord than to trust in man.
⁹ It is better to take refuge in the Lord than to trust in princes.

¹⁰ All nations surrounded me; in the name of the Lord I cut them off!
¹¹ They surrounded me, surrounded me on every side; in the name of the Lord I cut them off!
¹² They surrounded me like bees; they went out like a fire among thorns; in the name of the Lord I cut them off!¹³ I was pushed hard, so that I was falling, but the Lord helped me.

¹⁴ The Lord is my strength and my song; he has become my salvation.
¹⁵ Glad songs of salvation are in the tents of the righteous: The right hand of the Lord does valiantly

,¹⁶ the right hand of the Lord exalts, the right hand of the Lord does valiantly!"

¹⁷ I shall not die, but I shall live, and recount the deeds of the Lord.
¹⁸ The Lord has disciplined me severely, but he has not given me over to death.

¹⁹ Open to me the gates of righteousness, that I may enter through them and give thanks to the Lord.
²⁰ This is the gate of the Lord; the righteous shall enter through it.
²¹ I thank you that you have answered me and have become my salvation.
²² The stone that the builders rejected has become the cornerstone.
²³ This is the Lord's doing; it is marvelous in our eyes.
²⁴ This is the day that the Lord has made; let us rejoice and be glad in it.

²⁵ Save us, we pray, O Lord! O Lord, we pray, give us success!

²⁶ Blessed is he who comes in the name of the Lord! We bless you from the house of the Lord.

*²⁷ **The Lord is God, and he has made his light to shine upon us.
Bind the festal sacrifice with cords, up to the horns of the altar!***

*²⁸ **You are my God, and I will give thanks to you; you are my God; I will extol you.**
²⁹ **Oh give thanks to the Lord, for he is good; for his steadfast love endures forever!***

Abba….

Your Appointed Time with us begins this afternoon, and ends with the Sound of the Shofar tomorrow afternoon. So many things are happening right before our eyes. The world continues to change as much as we want it to stop. We call out to You, Yahuah, to help us to see You at work in the Land of the Living. Help us to be fully alive and to be participants in Your work.

We know that there is spiritual warfare being fought in our midst, in our cities, in our country. We know the battlefield can be as BIG as the whole world or as small as the distance between our two ears.

Father, forgive our shortcomings: words spoken without thought; thoughts in our minds without grace or empathy for others. Alone, we are but nefesh (flesh); but by Your grace and mercy, we have Your Spirit indwelling us.

*Holy Spirit, we cry out to You to come and fill each one who can pray these words. **Fill** and **Equip** and **Use** and **Send** us out to the fields white with harvest. Help us help You in the days ahead. You are not willing that any should perish but that all should come to repentance.*

Make our hearts tender toward one another, and toward You, and toward those we have not yet met. Send us forth fully dressed in the spiritual armor which You have provided: the breastplate of righteousness, the helmet of salvation, the belt of truth, shoes of peace and the sword of the Spirit. We ask, this day, that Your NESHAMA (BREATH OF LIFE) fill each and every one reading these words… those in agreement with this prayer. Help us be fully equipped to face each day and to represent You properly, and to love others and do unto to them as we would like to have them do unto us.

In the Mighty Name of Yeshua, our Salvation….

YOM KIPPUR

The most Holy Day on the Jewish calendar. A day of fasting and denying of one's selfish needs.

On my calendar and I hope on yours, this is a day of anticipation. What can we expect? What have you decided to do this day? Fast from food? If you have, enjoy it. Don't mourn for food, you can deny your flesh for one day. Feast on God's Word instead (drink plenty of water). Sit quietly with Him. Turn your face toward Him alone. After a few hours, you will begin to hear your own heartbeat... and... that *Still Small Voice*.

The trumpet has been blown and the weeds have been pulled out of your field. The King is there, waiting to meet with you. It is your day in the courtroom with God. You can ask Him anything. Listen for the long trumpet sound. It is called Tekiah Gadola. It is the sound of the verdict of the Court.

After these 40 days of watching the harvest come in, and the weeds being pulled out, you will feel God's smile coming your way. The accuser of the brethren will be there too, but you have attended to your repentance. You can say of Yeshua, "He is my Defense". You are not afraid. You know Him and you know what He has done for you. HalleluYah!

Abba...

After these forty days... I am not afraid to go Court. I am looking forward to it. No more blood, no more ashes, no more leading a scapegoat out of the camp to send my sins away – temporarily.

There is never one more sin sacrifice to be made. It is finished. The temple sacrificial system is done. We are the Temple of God. We are living stones making up Your Temple. It is from us that praise and thanksgiving arises to our God.

You dwell in me. You in me, and me in You. What will You and I do on this day of Yom Kippur, to celebrate the Atonement I have in You?

I will sit at Your table, and open Your Word, and hold it in my hands, and listen for Your voice, and hear Your words tell me again - that You love me.

I am Yours and You are the Judge finding in my favor in the midst of this ungodly world. Messiah has not only paid my fine, but is silencing the enemy on my behalf. Today, I expect the enemy of my soul to be bound and gagged.

Indeed, this is the day the LORD has made. I will rejoice in it and be glad. I have found both Peace and Justice with my Savior, and together, we celebrate Atonement.

Suddenly, a Still Small Voice is heard:

"Now, is the time you will see what I will do on behalf of those

who have joined the-journey-of-repentance."

THE TIME IS NOW!

By Myra Emslie

Chaos.
Everywhere, chaos.
Sea to shining sea, chaos.
The LORD our God is allowing the evil one to play his best hand.
And we see chaos,
hatred,
demonstrations about nothing,
vehement anger over contrived issues,
children stirred up to wrath,
Congress haggling over nothing
pouting to get their own way,
strife fanned to flame over the airwaves,
leadership allowing mouths to scream in anger.

Is this the coming of Your Kingdom, O God?
Is Your coming bringing such unrest and strife?
Have Your enemies begun to flee before You, as we have prayed?

"I, even I, AM digging up the hard soil.
I, even I, AM uprooting strongholds long-buried in the earth.
I, even I, AM pulling the devil up by the hair.
I, even I, AM forcing him to play his best hand.
Evil has simmered below the surface for thousands of years.
It has bubbled over many times with bloodshed and hatred and
defaming of My Name!
Even My Holy Word is smeared with blood."

"NOW!" Says the LORD of Hosts!
"Hear the blast of the trumpets calling you to battle!"

"NOW!" Says the LORD of Hosts!
"The fullness of time has come!"

"NOW!" Says the LORD of Hosts!
"For the ark of MY COVENANT goes before you!"

"NOW!" Says the LORD of Hosts!
"March into MY battle in your gleaming suits of armor with
the Sword of the Spirit held high!"

"NOW!" Says the LORD of Hosts!
"Watch the wall of Jericho come tumbling down!"

"You have called on Me to rise up!
You have called on Me to scatter My enemies!
You have called on Me to show Myself strong!
This is MY ANSWER!" Says the LORD.
"So, YOU rise up!
YOU, My righteous ones, rejoice and be glad.
DO NOT be dismayed or frightened or confused.
READ My Word and see the record!
When I arise, My power is without question.
I DO scatter all those who hate Me!
I DO cause them to flee, screaming in terror.
You are about to see the Power and Strength and Righteousness and
Glory of YOUR GOD
being poured out on the earth!
So, rejoice, my beloved ones!
Rejoice!
For your King is coming and you will see Him, just as He has promised!"

"Now, enter the battle in the power of the Holy Spirit.
Don't just sit there, dismayed and worried.
YOU rise up in FAITH and listen for the sound of the trumpets.
For the battle is MINE
And the victory is MINE
and the earth is MINE
and YOU are MINE!
Time is in MY hands and Time is full!
Look up and lift up your heads, because your redemption draws near!"

Amen.
Even so, come Lord Jesus!

Psalm 68:1-3
Psalm 74:22-23
Luke 21:28
Numbers 10:33-36
Revelation 22:20

EPILOGUE
Final Note from the Author

Well, we did it. We are at the end of this 40-day-journey of Repentance. I hope you have enjoyed this time and have learned something along the way. Again, I ask, what would happen if all those who proclaim the name of Jesus would take a journey such as this?

Repentance is the key to the Kingdom. We can't get in without it. Repentance is like your dad giving you the keys to his car. Without the keys the car won't go anywhere. Without repentance in our lives, we aren't going very far into the Kingdom of God.

Learning that *Repentance* is turning around and changing your mind - about God - is essential to our walk. *Changing your mind* about who God is, happens to be the other half of *asking for forgiveness*. Oftentimes we get the cart before the horse. We want God to forgive us without the repentance, and we end up not really knowing Him.

Try this experiment. Put your hands out in front of you... palms facing and about six inches apart. Move your hands in a turning motion, like you were holding an imaginary ball. Move that ball back and forth and all around, and keep your eyes on it. That represents your *universe* and your *mind*. We are effectively saying, "I'll hold my universe in my own hands." We do what we want to do, when we want to do it.

A good portion of our lives are spent entertaining different gods. Most of the time we think we are 'God', doing as we please and doing what is right in our own eyes! A quick look at our country, our beloved America, will explain that remark. Everything came to a stop in March of 2020.

Now as I write this, sports teams are playing in empty stadiums, theaters remain closed, schools are online, businesses are only beginning to open up, doctors are not in agreement, politics are dividing families, people don't know what to believe from the news, churches are all but padlocked, and people are hiding behind masks. We are discovering that we are not God!

Repentance is ***as-individual-as-individuals-are-individual***! You are not like anyone else. You are unique and you are special. Getting to know God through the other end of forgiveness, i.e. repentance is saying to Him… "Let me let You love me."

The cycle goes like this: Repentance, Forgiveness, Thanksgiving, Praise and Worship to the One who sets us free.

*If My people who are called by My Name will humble themselves and pray and **turn from their wicked ways** (i.e. repent), then will I hear from heaven and heal their land. II Chronicles 7:14.*

I wish you joy for the rest of your journey!

Susan Miller

Other books available from Semicolon Publishing – Loveland, Colorado

Make a Difference ~

Forty Days of Repentance

by Susan Miller

MESSIAH SERIES:

7 Miles with Messiah ~

Revelation in Emmaus ~ Finding Truth in Prophecy and History

by Myra Emslie & Susan Miller

7 Days with Messiah ~

Things I Didn't Learn in Sunday School ~ Meetings with My Forever Friend

by Susan Miller

7 Hours with Messiah ~

Changing Everything Forever ~ His Story

by Myra Emslie

SYMPHONY OF WARFARE SERIES:

Book 1   Symphony of Warfare ~

Invisible Power of Prayer

by Myra Emslie

Book 2   Symphony of Warfare ~

Fill Us with Courage

by Myra Emslie

Book 3   Symphony of Warfare ~

Call US to Attention

by Myra Emslie

www.ingramcontent.com/pod-product-compliance
Lightning Source LLC
Chambersburg PA
CBHW081226040426
42445CB00016B/1902